THE CIVIL WAR
UP CLOSE

THE CIVIL WAR UP CLOSE

Thousands of Curious, Obscure, and Fascinating Facts about the War America Could Never Win

Donald Cartmell

BARNES
& NOBLE

NEW YORK

This book is dedicated to **MORDECAI CARTMELL**, who served as a captain in the 11th Virginia Cavalry, a part of General Tom Rosser's Laurel Brigade. Cited for meritorious service at Brandy Station, where he had three horses killed under him, he was promoted to captain for his performance at Upperville, Virginia, in June 1863. Captain Cartmell was killed while leading his squadron on a charge at Sangster's Station, Virginia, on December 17, 1863. His body was returned to Winchester for burial by his brother Thomas who also served with the 11th Virginia. He was buried in the family cemetery beside the Round Hill Presbyterian Church outside Winchester, Virginia. He also had a brother, Robert Cartmell, who served as a courier on Robert E. Lee's staff.

CONTENTS

Introduction **13**

Part One: The Politicians
15

**Chapter 1: The Good, the Bad, and
the Ugly of the Wartime Governors** **19**

State Politics in a Time of War 19

    Zebulon Vance: Champion of the Tar Heel State 21

    Oliver P. Morton: Dictator of Indiana 22

    Honest John Letcher: Unionist Governor of Virginia 23

    Horatio Seymour: Godfather of the New York City Draft Riot 25

    Joseph E. Brown: Ploughboy From Georgia 26

    Claiborne Jackson: Governor in Exile 27

**Chapter 2: The Best and the Worst
of the Presidential Cabinets** **31**

How They Were Chosen 31

    William Seward: Lincoln's Prime Minister 32

    John C. Breckinridge: Too Little Too Late 35

    Edwin Stanton: Aspiring to the Supreme Court 36

    Judah Benjamin: Friend to the President 38

    Salmon Chase: Old Greenbacks 40

Simon Cameron and Alexander Stephens: The Thorns 41

Chapter 3: Global Aspects of the Civil War 43

The Confederacy's Only Foreign War 43

Mexico, Part One: Stillbirth of an Empire 45

Mexico, Part Two: Napoleon in the New World 46

Japan, Part One: War in the Pacific 47

Japan, Part Two: Back to Shimonoseki 48

Russia: A Gesture of Goodwill 48

Oddities: Poland and the Vatican 50

Part Two: The Generals
53

Chapter 4: The Best and the Worst
of the Senior Citizen Generals 57

What Happened to the Old Guard 57

Winfield Scott: Old Fuss and Feathers 58

David Twiggs: All I Have Is in the South 59

John Wool: Hero of Troy 61

William Harney: Indian Fighter 62

James Ripley: Ripley Van Winkle 65

Chapter 5: The Top Generals of the Confederacy 67

The Perils of Seniority 67

The First Crisis in Command: Joe Johnston Is Wounded 69

The Second Crisis in Command: P.G.T. Beauregard Goes AWOL 71

The Third Crisis in Command: Utter Defeat for Braxton Bragg 73

The Fourth Crisis in Command: Joe Johnston Retreats Again 74

Chapter 6: The Civil War Hall of Shame: Commanders
With Bad Timing, Bad Judgment, and Bad Luck 77

Edward Baker: Blind Man's Bluff 77

Jefferson C. Davis: Getting Away With Murder 79

Nathan Shanks Evans: Drunk and Disorderly 80

James Ledlie: Bombed at the Crater 81

John Newton: Engineering Defeat in Florida 83

Thomas Selfridge: Best Swimmer in the Navy 84

Earl Van Dorn: Victim of Love 85

Felix Zollicoffer: Nearsighted Newspaperman 87

Part Three: The Fighting
89

**Chapter 7: The Most Influential
Battles of the Civil War** **93**

Manassas: The First Major Victory of the War 93

Fort Donelson: Birthplace of Unconditional Surrender Grant 95

Glorieta Pass: On to San Francisco! 97

New Orleans: Largest City in the Confederacy Is Lost 98

The Seven Days' Battle: What Might Have Been 99

Antietam: Spearhead for the Emancipation Proclamation 102

Atlanta: Gone With the Wind 103

Five Forks: Road to Final Victory 105

**Chapter 8: The Most Influential
Campaigns of the Civil War** **107**

1861, Western Virginia: Lee's First Retreat 107

1862, the Shenandoah Valley: Triumph of Jackson's Foot Cavalry 109

1863, Vicksburg Campaign: The Greatness of Ulysses S. Grant 111

1864, the Shenandoah Valley Revisited: Horror in the Valley 112

1865, Appomattox: Final Retreat 114

Chapter 9: Mysteries of the Deep **117**

Submarine Warfare: Early Attempts, Failures, and Death 117

Union Submariners: An Alligator in the James River 120

Success at Last: Adventures of the Singer Submarine Corps 122

Part Four: The Medicine
127

Chapter 10: The Worst Doctors in the Union Army **131**

Eating Disorders and the Hospital Fund 131

Edward Boemer: Misapplication of Stores and Money 132

Enoch Blanchard: The Case of the Illegal Sweet Potatoes 133

Alonza Eisenlord: Innocent of All Charges 134

Drunken Doctors in Operation 135

Luther G. Thomas: Drunk on Duty 135

William H. Lakeman: Never Mix Brandy and Opium 137

William B. Hezlep: Never Too Drunk to Operate 138

Strange but True Doctor Stories 139

Charles E. Briggs: Doctor or Veterinarian 140

George H. Mitchell: Three-Time Loser 141

Edward Flynn: The Sting 142

Chapter 11: Sick and Wounded Generals in the Confederate Army **145**

Thomas Fenton Toon: North Carolina's Finest 145

Daniel Adams: Left for Dead 147

Nathan Bedford Forrest: Riding With the Devil 148

Dick Ewell and Francis Nicholls: Losing an Arm and a Leg 149

Lee, Beauregard, and Bragg: The Strain of Command 151

Garnett, Hunton, and Kemper: The Horsemen of Pickett's Charge ... 154

Joe Johnston: Honorable Mention 155

Part Five: The Aftermath
157

Chapter 12: The Monumental Battle of Gettysburg **161**

Bachelder's Battlefield 161

    The Copse of Trees: Monumental Battles at The Angle 163

    Little Round Top: Remembering Strong Vincent 164

    Longstreet's Revenge: Southern Strategy at Gettysburg 166

    Capital Connection: Monuments in Richmond and Washington 169

Chapter 13: Continuing
Controversies of the Civil War **171**

    Switched at Birth: The Last Prisoners of War 171

    The Fabrication of a Legend: Abraham Lincoln's Birth Cabin 172

    The Burning of Columbia: An Accident of War 174

    Black Confederates: A Modern-Day Phenomenon 175

    When Things Go Wrong: The Mass Hangings of 1862 178

Chapter 14: The Civil War in Poetry **181**

    Thomas Read: Sheridan's Wild Ride 181

    John Reuben Thompson: Dead Soldier Poems 185

    Paul Hamilton Hayne: Poet Laureate of the South 188

    Walt Whitman: Union Nurse, American Poet 192

Bibliography **195**

Index **203**

About the Author **209**

INTRODUCTION

The Civil War, more than any other event in American history, has forged our culture and our national identity. Not only did the Civil War end the practice of slavery, it also fostered a host of changes that altered the very fabric of American society. Things we now take for granted such as wartime draft, a national currency, a federal income tax, and standardized clothing sizes were instituted, for better and for worse, during the Civil War. While some of the changes were widely recognized, many more were hidden just beneath the surface. For example, the Fourteenth Amendment, which was ratified just after the war ended and intended to protect the civil rights of newly freed slaves, was rarely invoked until the 1960s. However, the amendment was utilized very successfully to enhance the legal rights of corporations, especially after the Supreme Court ruled that corporations had the same legal rights, under the due process clause, as a person. Like an iceberg, much of what occurred during the Civil War remains submerged. The submerged part is what this book will seek to uncover.

The Civil War Up Close will reexamine accepted theories with a fresh outlook and bring hard-hitting analysis to many of the accepted theories about the war. In addition, it is hoped this book will serve to motivate the reader to reevaluate long-held opinions through an exploration of lesser known but fascinating facts about the war and the people who won and lost it. The book is divided into five sections with each section providing a platform for delving into some of the murkier aspects of the war. The first section, The Politicians, examines some of the men who served as state governors and in the wartime presidential cabinets, as well as chronicling the first steps the United States took to becoming a global power. The second section, The Generals, brings to light some of the reasons that the Confederacy was unable to develop new generals, while such little known and regarded men as Ulysses S. Grant, William T. Sherman, and Phil Sheridan rose to prominence in the Union army. In addition, the chapter includes a discussion on senior citizen generals and a general Hall of Shame. The third section, The Fighting, examines the most influential battles and campaigns of the war and brings to light some little known facts about the rise of submarine warfare. The fourth section, The Medicine, explains why surgeons and doctors had such a difficult time rising to the many challenges that emerged during the war. And finally, the fifth section, The Aftermath, examines such things at the rivalry between the North and the South in building monuments to commemorate the war and some of the continuing controversies of the war.

There was one rule observed during the writing of *The Civil War Up Close*: Every section had to answer a question about some aspect of the Civil War that has been, for the most part, overlooked. Some examples include: What happened to the old guard? How close did the Confederacy come to obtaining European support? Who were the worst generals? And, who were the worst doctors? These questions and more will be answered in *The Civil War Up Close*.

PART ONE

THE POLITICIANS

Every student of the Civil War is familiar with the names of Abraham Lincoln, Robert E. Lee, and Ulysses S. Grant. These men, along with a handful of others, dominate the landscape of Civil War scholarship. However, there were dozens of other men who played significant roles in the military and economic efforts of the North and South. One example can be found by examining the roles played by a variety of state governors. Both Abraham Lincoln and Jefferson Davis relied heavily upon the efforts of state governors to keep their great war machines functioning properly. Men like Governor Oliver P. Morton of Illinois and Governor Zebulon Vance of North Carolina wielded tremendous power in their respective states and played a critical role in the outcome of the Civil War. Another group who wielded great influence during the war were the men chosen by Presidents Lincoln and Davis to serve as senior advisors in their wartime cabinets. Some, such as William Seward and Judah Benjamin, served their president well and performed great services, while others, such as Simon Cameron, were more interested in personal gain than in military victory. This section of the book will examine an assortment of these men who operated in and around the corridors of power, in an attempt to shed some light on their activities and explain their role in the war.

CHAPTER 1

THE GOOD, THE BAD, AND THE UGLY OF THE WARTIME GOVERNORS

State Politics in a Time of War

While the governments of Abraham Lincoln and Jefferson Davis have undergone close scrutiny for their behavior during the Civil War, it was the state governors that bore the brunt of trying to keep democracy afloat during wartime. This layer of government served as a buffer between the rapidly growing interests of the central government and the strong desire for local autonomy demanded by most citizens. State governors were also largely responsible for supplying men and raising armies. This was especially true early in the war when the first calls for troops were answered by state militias. Even later in the war, it was the responsibility of the states to raise volunteer regiments for the army. This is why each military unit had a state designation—for example, the 20th Maine. In addition, the governors were called upon to manage wartime economies that had to feed and equip thousands of soldiers in the field, while providing for the needs of the citizenry at home.

Most wartime governors in the North rose to meet this challenge. In Connecticut, Governor William Buckingham was asked to raise 10 companies of men at the start of the war; he raised 54. By the end of the war, Connecticut—a state with only 461,000 citizens and 80,000 eligible voters—sent 54,882 volunteers to the Union army. Governor Andrew Curtain of Pennsylvania organized a governor's conference in September 1862 to reaffirm the states' commitment to the war effort after President Lincoln had announced his intention to issue the Emancipation Proclamation. He also mobilized the state militia that helped stop General Lee's advance forces from crossing the Susquehanna River and marching into the state capital, Harrisburg, during the Gettysburg campaign. Governor Erastus Fairbanks of Vermont, a rich industrialist, deferred his own salary and used his business connections to secure a credit line for the purchase of war supplies, and Governor Samuel Kirkwood of Iowa organized the Northern Iowa Brigade to protect against Indian raids.

Jefferson Davis also found he could rely on many of his state governors to help the war effort. Governor Milledge Bonham of South Carolina impressed thousands of slaves to help build many of the coastal and harbor defenses that withstood three years of almost constant Union attacks, despite the fact that this made him very unpopular among wealthy and powerful slaveholders. In Louisiana, Thomas Moore governed the state while attempting to stay one step ahead of the invading Union army by moving the state capital from Baton Rouge to Opelousas and finally to Shreveport. When it became impossible for Florida governor John Milton to adequately supply state troops, he sent them on to Richmond to join the Confederate army, despite the fact that this left his home state largely undefended against Union incursions. Milton was so loyal to the cause that he committed suicide on April 1, 1865, rather than watch his beloved Confederacy fall.

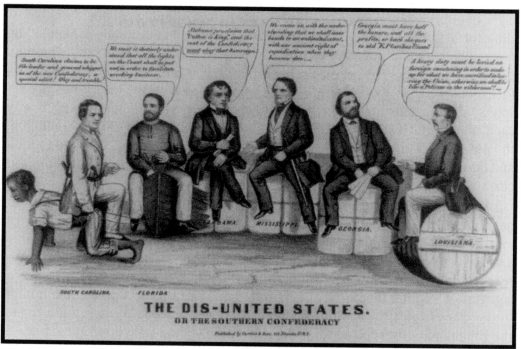

Confederate governors lampooned in a drawing published by Currier and Ives. (Library of Congress)

Zebulon Vance:
Champion of the Tar Heel State

While North Carolina did not produce a battlefield general that could compare with Robert E. Lee or Nathan Bedford Forrest, it did produce a governor whose contributions were almost as dramatic. This is how historian Glenn Tucker described Governor Zebulon Vance: "None sent more recruits...to Lee's man-hungry army than did Vance. None supplied it in greater measure with food, provender, and military goods. None to a greater degree inspired its soldiers with lofty motives and firmness to battle through to their last resource." In his

dealings with President Davis, Vance subscribed to the theory that it was his job to "fight the Yankees and fuss the Confederacy." Even during the depths of total war, Vance insisted upon maintaining the rule of law. While other state governments in the Confederacy either crumbled under the weight of war or succumbed to the whims of the Davis administration, the courts in North Carolina continued to function and it was the only Southern state which never suspended the writ of habeas corpus.

When the war began, Vance, who was serving as a congressman in Washington, returned home to take command of a volunteer company called the Rough and Ready Guards. Later, Vance was promoted to commander of the 26th North Carolina Infantry and led this unit at the battles of New Berne, Kinston, and

North Carolina governor Zebulon Vance, in later years. (Library of Congress)

Malvern Hill. While serving in Virginia, he was nominated for governor and easily won the election on August 6, 1862. One of the first things he did was appropriate $100,000 to set up hospitals throughout the state and to create a Soldier's Home to take care of soldiers in transit to and from Virginia. Vance also helped to increase the yearly harvest in corn and other foodstuffs by prohibiting the planting of any new tobacco or cotton crops. Furthermore, he pushed through a law prohibiting the distillation of liquor as a way to save tons of grain. After several months, however, he was forced to relent to pressure from Richmond and allow a government-run distillery to operate near Salisbury for the purpose of making medicinal whiskey.

Perhaps the most interesting example of Vance's innovative approach to wartime governing was his investment, on behalf of the state, in the blockade-runner *Ad Vance*. Launched in July 1862, the *Ad Vance* made 20 successful voyages before being captured by the USS *Santiago de Cuba* in September 1864. Among other things, this investment netted the North Carolina and the Confederacy more than 250,000 uniforms, 50,000 blankets, and other supplies, in preparation for the Gettysburg campaign.

Vance also restructured the state economy in other ways. For example, North Carolina increased production of wool, cotton, and leather goods so that it was able to export large quantities to other states. In fact, while many soldiers in the Army of Northern Virginia had to beg, borrow, or steal proper footwear and clothing, North Carolina's troops were always the best dressed and equipped in the army.

Oliver P. Morton: Dictator of Indiana

Although Oliver P. Morton is best known for his key role in the passage of the Fifteenth Amendment, it was his activities early in the Civil War that earned him the nickname as "The Great War Governor." Under Morton's guidance, Indiana met or exceeded every quota levied by President Lincoln, resulting in the recruitment of 150,000 men and boys to fight in the Union army by the end of the war. Morton also

Oliver P. Morton, "The Great War Governor" of Illinois. (Library of Congress)

bolstered the morale of his citizens by delivering inspirational addresses throughout the state: "We must…cling to the idea that we are a nation, one and indivisible…. We must therefore, do no act, we must tolerate no act, we must concede no idea or theory that looks to or involves the dismemberment of the nation."

Morton's biggest test was in 1862 when the Democrats took control of the Indiana legislature. After this occurred, the *Indianapolis Daily State Sentinel* asserted that the new general assembly would "hog-tie" and "horse-whip" Governor Morton. When Democrats attempted to pass a military bill that would severely limit his authority and demanded the immediate retraction of the "wicked, inhuman and unholy" Emancipation Proclamation in exchange for continued state support of the war, Morton convinced the Republican members of the legislature to leave the state. Lacking a quorum, the legislative session came to an end without the passage of any bills and left Morton as the virtual dictator of the state.

Because no appropriation or revenue bills had been passed before the legislative session's premature end, Morton faced the daunting task of finding some means to finance the state until the next election cycle in 1864. Against all odds, Morton succeeded in keeping the state solvent by borrowing money on his own assurances, obtaining loans from bankers, and by cajoling a $250,000 grant from the Lincoln administration. When told there was no law that allowed the Federal government to help Morton out of his predicament, Secretary of War Edwin Stanton declared: "By god, I will find a law." In all, Morton was able to raise more than a million dollars to keep the state government in operation. Of this, the vast majority was used for the benefit of the soldiers in the field and their dependents at home. However, for Morton's gambit to succeed, he had to win reelection or face personal financial ruin. Fortunately for him, his tireless efforts were rewarded, and he was reelected, despite the fact that his candidacy was unconstitutional (due to term limits) and that the soldiers from Indiana serving in the army were not allowed to vote. With the help of a new Republican majority, the general assembly was able to resume its proper role within the state government and Morton was able to repay all the loans that were issued under his name.

Honest John Letcher:
Unionist Governor of Virginia

Despite the fact that he was a delegate at Virginia's constitutional convention in 1850 and served four terms in Congress, few knew what to expect from newly elected Governor John Letcher when the secession crisis hit Virginia in 1860. First of all, Letcher was a Unionist who had refused to endorse secession until President Lincoln's call for troops on April 15, 1861. And secondly, although he had been given the nickname "Honest John" for his opposition to governmental extravagance, Letcher had a terrible reputation as an alcoholic whose "face was perpetually red from drink." According to historian Douglas Southall Freeman, "Everyone in the state knew that a visit to the governor's office would include a trip with Letcher to a liquor-laden sideboard."

However, once Virginia decided to join the Confederacy, Letcher worked quickly to form an alliance with Jefferson Davis's fledgling government. He sent Virginia militiamen to capture the valuable munitions factory at Harper's Ferry and the Gosport Navy Yard, home of the steamship *Merrimack* (which was subsequently converted into the ironclad CSS *Virginia*). Letcher also placed all Virginia regiments under Confederate control and offered Richmond as the permanent capital of the Confederacy. On May 29, 1861, Letcher welcomed President Jefferson Davis to Richmond and presented him with a large house at the corner of Twelfth and Clay streets—soon to be known as the Confederate White House. By his actions,

The White House of the Confederacy, home of President Jefferson Davis during the Civil War. (National Archives)

Letcher made sure that the fate of Virginia and the Confederacy would be inexorably intertwined.

Letcher was also instrumental in bringing forward two men who would soon join the vanguard of Confederate military officers. Letcher nominated Robert E. Lee as commander of Virginia's military forces and also submitted the name of a little-known VMI instructor, Thomas J. Jackson (previously a brevet major in the regular army), for a commission as infantry colonel. Despite cries of "Who is Major Jackson?" the convention accepted his appointment and, at Letcher's direction, gave him command of the Virginia troops in Harper's Ferry.

Letcher also played a critical role in an incident that almost caused Jackson to resign from the army very early in the war. Displaying his usual zeal, Jackson decided his men would spend the winter of 1861–62 campaigning in western Virginia. Eventually, even the tenacious Jackson had to give in to the elements and withdraw his men to Winchester. However, he left a small force, commanded by General William Loring, near Romney, Virginia (now West Virginia), to hold the ground that had been captured. This greatly aggravated Loring, who already felt that Jackson had been favoring his own brigade throughout the cold and bitter winter campaign and referred to them derisively as "Jackson's pet lambs." Loring then circulated a petition that was signed by 11 of his officers complaining that the conditions at Romney were "the most disagreeable and unfavorable that could be imagined" and forwarded it Richmond. When President Davis agreed with the petitioners and directed Secretary of War Judah Benjamin to countermand Loring's orders, Jackson fired off an angry letter of his own.

Jackson felt so strongly that it would undercut his authority if officers in his command could defy his orders by appealing to Richmond that he submitted his resignation to President Davis. However, Jackson hedged his bet by also sending a personal letter to his good friend and mentor Governor Letcher. According to Jackson, the secretary of war was trying "to control military operations in detail from [his] desk at a distance." As Jackson had anticipated, Letcher made a vigorous protest to Secretary Benjamin, who agreed to postpone acceptance of Jackson's resignation until after Letcher had time to persuade Jackson to remain in the army. Jackson remained firm until Letcher convinced him that the South would be greatly demoralized by his resignation. Jackson replied, "If my retiring from the Army would produce that effect upon our country, I of course would not desire to leave the service." Although he had no way of knowing that Jackson would one day become a great general, Letcher performed a great service for the Confederacy by securing the services of the man who would come to known as "Stonewall." For his part, Loring was transferred to Georgia and served out the rest of the Civil War in relative obscurity.

Horatio Seymour:
Godfather of the New York City Draft Riot

For the first two years of the war, Abraham Lincoln enjoyed almost unlimited support from the governors in the North, as all but Delaware's William Burton were fellow Republicans. However, he knew that his honeymoon was coming to an end when Ohio, New York, and New Jersey all elected Democratic governors in late 1862. Of these, Lincoln knew that New York's Horatio Seymour posed the most complicated problem, because he had run on a platform rebuking the Emancipation Proclamation as "a proposal for the butchery of women and children, for scenes of lust and rapine, and of arson and murder." Although he vowed to support the war effort in his election campaign, Seymour held a slightly different opinion in 1860. "If it be true that slavery must be abolished to save this Union, then the people of the South should be allowed to withdraw themselves from the government which cannot give them the protection guaranteed by its terms."

At a time when New York City was filled with unsettling rumors about the upcoming military draft and many were outraged over the $300 exemption clause, Seymour attended a "Peace and Reunion" convention in the city. More than 30,000

New York State governor Horatio Seymour, inciting a crowd at City Hall Park in New York City. (Library of Congress)

New Yorkers jammed their way into City Hall Park to see an assortment of politicians (including Seymour) proclaim that "the war cannot succeed." Seymour went on to say, "We have been beaten. We cannot conquer the South." It is no wonder that, a day after the first list of names to be drafted was printed in the New York papers, the city exploded into violence. When the riot erupted, Seymour ignored advice to react strongly and instead attempted a policy of conciliation. When the riot spiraled out of control, Seymour had to admit his error and allow the army to enter the city and quell the riot.

Seymour followed this up by complaining loudly and bitterly that the Conscription Act was unconstitutional and that the draft in New York should be suspended until the Supreme Court ruled on the case. Despite Seymour's recalcitrance, the draft in New York proceeded with little additional difficulty. Seymour's activities did tremendous damage to the Union war effort. His failure to cooperate with General Dix in enforcing the draft necessitated the withdrawal of thousands of troops from the front lines to keep the peace in New York City, and some charged that this allowed General Lee to detach some of his men to Georgia where they helped win the battle of Chickamauga. In addition, when President Lincoln issued a call for 12,000 "one hundred days' men" to thwart a Confederate attack that threatened Washington in 1864, Seymour delayed so long that the men never saw service at the front.

When Seymour was nominated for a second term, the Lincoln administration did everything in its power to thwart his reelection. To prevent fraudulent voting, 3,000 additional troops were sent to New York City under the command of General Benjamin Butler, a staunch Republican and Lincoln supporter. In addition, several Democratic agents sent to assist soldiers in voting were arrested and charged with forgery and several large boxes of what were alleged to be illegal ballots that had already been forwarded to New York were seized. When the election was finally over, Seymour lost by a mere 9,000 votes to Reuben E. Fenton, a Republican and an avowed abolitionist. President Lincoln was now able breathe a little easier knowing that he could once again count on the full support of the powerful industrial and military capabilities of New York State.

Joseph E. Brown: Ploughboy From Georgia

Despite coming from a humble background, having little in the way of personal charisma, and not being particularly likable, Joe Brown rose to become the only man to be elected governor of Georgia four times. He also served, at various times, as a circuit judge, state senator, chief justice of the state supreme court, and U.S. senator. He was able to win elections because of what he said and what he did, not because of who he was or who he represented. In fact, he was derisively referred to as "The Ploughboy" before the war, because he came from a non-slaveholding family. After Abraham Lincoln was elected president, Brown was one of the most eloquent advocates of secession. Brown asserted that "the rights of the South, and the institution of slavery, are not endangered by the triumph of Mr. Lincoln, the man; but they are in imminent danger from the triumph of the powerful party which he represents, and of the fanatical abolition sentiment which brought him into power."

Brown was not afraid to back up his words with actions, as when he ordered the seizure of Federal forts in Pulaski and Jackson and personally seized the Federal arsenal in Augusta before the firing on Fort Sumter. However, Brown made it very clear, even at this early point in the war, that his first priority was what was best for

Georgia—not what was best for the Confederacy. He insisted that only he had the authority to appoint officers for regiments raised in Georgia and made sure only units that volunteered through his office were allowed to take state-owned weapons. Brown also refused to turn over any weapons or munitions seized from Federal armories until after the Georgia militia had taken what it needed.

Disagreements between Brown and President Jefferson Davis's administration grew larger after the Conscription Act was passed in early 1862. Brown believed the Act was unconstitutional, and he informed President Davis that he would not "consent to have anything to do with the enrollment of conscripts in this State." To emphasize his point, Brown appointed thousands of men to hastily created governmental positions to shield them from service in the army. Brown again locked horns with the Richmond authorities when President Davis was given the authority to suspend the writ of habeas corpus in areas "under threat of attack from the enemy." Brown responded by denouncing the law as a step towards military despotism: "What will we have gained when we have achieved our independence...if in our efforts to do so, we have...lost Constitutional Liberty at home?"

By 1864, Brown's clashes with Davis were so caustic that many thought he was deliberately seeking to hurt the Confederate war effort. Even those who gave Brown the benefit of the doubt were convinced that his never-ending efforts to defend state sovereignty did more harm than good. Late in the war Brown joined fellow Georgians Vice President Alexander Stephens and ex-general Robert Toombs in proposing a series of resolutions urging the people of Georgia to put pressure on the government to end the war. However, after doing this, Brown found he had stepped over the line. Not only were his efforts almost universally condemned at home, Georgia regiments at the front passed resolutions of their own, publicly condemning him. Governor Brown eventually gave up his running battle with the Davis administration when Union forces commanded by General Sherman tore through his home state and rendered his quixotic defense of state sovereignty, in the midst of civil war, a moot point.

Claiborne Jackson: Governor in Exile

Missouri's antebellum history was fraught with violence and strife. Born as a result of the Missouri Compromise, the state was plunged into turmoil during the fight over slavery in "Bloody Kansas." Claib Jackson made a name for himself in 1855 by leading the group of "border ruffians" into Lawrence, Kansas, to vote in favor of legalizing slavery. By the time Jackson and his men had left, the pro-slavery forces had won the vote by a count of 781 to 253. A congressional investigation later determined that only 232 of the pro-slavery votes were legal. In 1860, Jackson ran for governor of the state. Despite the fact that he had pledged to support a pro-Union platform, he immediately began campaigning for secession after he won the election. In his acceptance speech, Jackson said: "The destiny of the slave-holding States of the Union is one and the same.... Common origin, pursuits, tastes, manners and customs...bind together in one brotherhood the States of the South." With that utterance, Jackson brought civil war to Missouri.

Confident that he could lead Missouri into the Confederacy, Jackson called for a "convention to consider the question of secession and the adoption of measures to vindicate the sovereignty of the State." However, Jackson was outfoxed by Republican congressman Frank Blair, who arranged for the convention to be moved to strongly pro-Union St. Louis. Much to Jackson's dismay, none of the 99 elected delegates would publicly favor separating from the Union. Jackson's next gambit was to take control of the St. Louis police force and to mobilize units of the pro-South Missouri militia. The big prize was the Federal arsenal in St. Louis—the largest in all the slave states, containing 60,000 muskets, several artillery pieces, and other assorted weaponry. Jackson knew that whoever controlled the arsenal controlled St. Louis and that whoever controlled St. Louis would control the state. Again, Frank Blair, with the help of newly arrived reinforcements commanded by Captain (soon to be General) Nathaniel Lyon, was able to thwart

Currier and Ives print depicting the Union's general Nathaniel Lyon chasing Governor Claib Jackson and General Sterling Price out of Missouri. (Library of Congress)

Jackson's plan by going on the offensive and attacking the militia camp outside the city. Caught by surprise, the 700 militiamen surrendered without firing a single shot. After the disaster, M. Jeff Thompson, one of the militia officers, confronted Jackson. "Governor, before I leave, I wish to tell you the two qualities of a soldier.... One of them is Common Sense and the other is Courage—and By God! You have neither."

In the wake of his defeat in St. Louis, Governor Jackson returned to the state capital in Jefferson City and issued a proclamation calling for 50,000 men to join him to help repel the "invaders." He also authorized the borrowing of a million dollars to raise a state army and appropriated what was in the state treasury for his own personal use before leaving for Boonville with the remnants of the pro-South militia. In his absence a provisional government of Missouri was formed, and a new pro-Union governor was elected. Jackson held his own convention in Neosho, near the Arkansas border, and finally got his wish when they enacted an ordinance of secession on November 3, 1861. Although political and military control of the state remained in Union hands throughout the war,

Missouri was formally admitted into the Confederacy on November 28, 1861, and the state was represented in Richmond by a government in exile. A year later, Governor-in-exile Claib Jackson died from stomach cancer. While Jackson's attempt to "Southernize" Missouri was unsuccessful, his exploits as governor were memorialized in the song "The War in Missouri in 1861," composed by an unknown Union soldier:

> *Come all you jolly Union boys, the truth to you I'll tell,*
> *About old Governor Jackson, of whom you know so well.*
> *He undertook a project and he didn't quite succeed,*
> *In forcing of Missouri from the Union to secede.*
> *Old Claiborne for to show his hand, he swore he'd cut a dash.*
> *He stepped up to the treasury and stole away the cash.*

CHAPTER 2

THE BEST AND THE WORST OF THE PRESIDENTIAL CABINETS

How They Were Chosen

Despite being favored to win the Republican nomination for president in 1860, a disappointed William Seward accepted Abraham Lincoln's offer to become a member of his cabinet as secretary of state. Lincoln also tapped his other main rivals for the presidential nomination when choosing the rest of his cabinet. Ex-Whig Edward Bates, a congressman from Missouri, was chosen as the new attorney general and Senator Simon Cameron of Pennsylvania was appointed secretary of war. Cameron's nomination irked Lincoln because his convention managers had promised Cameron the appointment without Lincoln's permission. After toying with the idea of reneging on the promise, Lincoln relented—despite Cameron's checkered reputation, due to his penchant for dishonest business dealings. For the final post, secretary of the treasury, Lincoln wanted Salmon Chase because of his reputation as leader of the "Iron-Back" Republicans who opposed any concessions for the South. Seward balked at Chase's appointment, but backed down when Lincoln threatened to nominate William Dayton in his stead. When all was said and done, Lincoln had chosen a cabinet filled with political rivals and men who had opposed his nomination. While Lincoln's choices put the best and brightest men in the Republican Party at his disposal, it also guaranteed that Lincoln would have a difficult time getting these men to work together and to accept him as their leader.

Although Lincoln had to deal with Republican party politics while choosing his cabinet, President Jefferson Davis, who had not campaigned for the job and did not have any favors to reciprocate, kept geography foremost in his mind when choosing advisors. When he arrived in Montgomery, Alabama, to take office, Davis met his new vice president, Alexander Stephens, who had been given that position at the behest of Robert Toombs, primarily because he was from Georgia. Toombs, the new secretary of state, had been instrumental in leading Georgia out of the Union and in creating the Confederate constitution. Davis also had to make sure that the remaining states in the Confederacy were represented in his cabinet. Christopher Memminger, a banker and chairman of the committee that drafted the Confederate constitution, was chosen to represent South Carolina as secretary of the treasury. At the prompting of state officials, Alabama was represented by Leroy P. Walker as secretary of war despite the fact that Walker had never before held an executive position. Davis chose his friend from Louisiana, Judah Benjamin, to be attorney general and rounded out his cabinet by selecting Stephen Mallory (secretary of the navy) and John Reagan (postmaster-general)

Alexander Stephens was chosen to be President Jefferson Davis's vice president primarily because he was from Georgia. (Library of Congress)

of Florida and Texas, respectively. When he was finished, Davis had selected representatives from every Southern state that had seceded, except his own home state of Mississippi. Although Davis's appointments were well received throughout the Confederacy, there was one significant criticism: Davis had left out most of the hard-core "fire-eaters" who had led the charge for secession and, instead, had selected men who had supported former Vice President John Breckinridge, the relatively moderate Southern Right's Democrat, in the 1860 presidential election.

William Seward: Lincoln's Prime Minister

The man who probably became the most influential presidential advisor during the war was Lincoln's secretary of state William Seward. Born in a small village in upstate New York, William Seward led a long and diverse career in politics that twice brought him to the brink of the presidency. In 1856 Seward was persuaded not to accept the Republican nomination because it was widely believed that the newly formed party could not win. Throughout the rest of his life, Seward believed that if he had accepted that nomination he would have won the presidency. Seward bided his time prior to the 1860 presidential election by traveling to Europe. In England Seward was welcomed by Queen Victoria, Lord Palmerston, Lord Lansdowne, Lord Granville, the Duke of Sutherland, and Lord John Russell. In other parts of Europe, Seward was welcomed by King Louis Napoleon, King Victor Emmanuel, Count Cavour, and Pope Pius IX. The main reason for Seward's grand reception was because it was believed he would succeed James Buchanan in the White House.

As the most prominent Republican in the country, Seward was the front-runner for the presidential nomination in 1860 and had a wide lead (173 of the needed 234 delegates) after the first ballot was taken at the party convention. Seward's confidence remained high even after little-known Abraham Lincoln rocketed to second place in the second ballot (Seward led only 184 votes to 181). Only when he read the results of the third ballot—a unanimous decision in favor of Lincoln—did Seward begin to realize that his dreams of becoming president would remain unfulfilled. Seward's downfall was his reputation as a radical Republican. After his famous "Irrepressible Conflict" speech, Seward was seen by many as too extreme to win any of the states in the lower North (Indiana, Illinois, Pennsylvania, and New Jersey)—states the Republicans had carried in 1856 and would need again in 1860.

Seward quickly rejected Lincoln's offer for the vice presidency. Instead, Seward believed that as the leader of the Republican party he should be the one to determine the composition of the cabinet. Seward had in mind a Lincoln presidency modeled after the British government, with Seward himself taking the role of prime minister. However, Lincoln had no intention of abdicating the presidency in favor of Seward and his political cronies. At the beginning of the administration, Seward was adamant that Fort Sumter should be evacuated. To Seward's dismay, Lincoln

William Seward finished second to Abraham Lincoln in the 1860 Republican Convention and served as Lincoln's secretary of state throughout the war. (National Archives)

totally disregarded his advice. In doing so, Lincoln firmly established that he was going to be the person who made the difficult decisions. While Seward and Lincoln did not see eye to eye early in the war, the two were able to form a bond that was strongly reinforced by Seward's deft handling of the *Trent* affair.

One of the most pervasive myths of the Civil War is the belief that if the Confederate army had been able to win a battle on Northern soil England would have granted the Confederacy formal recognition. However, England was very proud of its role in suppressing the slave trade and of abolishing slavery in the West Indies; as long as the South had fought to keep slavery legal, England and the rest of Europe would have remained officially neutral. The real danger point, in terms of European interference, was the tumultuous period at the beginning of the war. Just after the bombardment of Fort Sumter, the Confederacy sent a delegation of commissioners to meet with Lord Russell. Soon after, Queen Elizabeth issued a Proclamation of Neutrality that recognized the Confederacy as a belligerent power. As such, the Confederacy had the right, under international law, to contract loans and purchase arms from neutral countries and to commission commerce raiders on the high seas. The situation heated up when the steamer *Trent*, carrying two Confederate ministers (James Mason and John Slidell) to France and England, was seized by Charles Wilkes, commander of the USS *San Jacinto*.

Wilkes's actions sparked an international incident that could have easily ended in war between the United States and Britain. Lord Palmerston sent an ultimatum to President Lincoln, demanding an official apology and the immediate release of the Confederate diplomats. After studying the situation, Secretary of State Seward argued that Wilkes had violated international law and that Mason and Slidell could be released without the official apology that Lincoln was loathe to make. Seward convinced the rest of the cabinet members, in a dramatic Christmas Day meeting, to endorse his plan, and President Lincoln, concluding that the United States should fight only one war at a time, concurred. The release of Mason and Slidell was perhaps Seward's finest hour as a statesman and not only served to puncture the "war bubble," but also left Anglo-American relations in better shape than they were before the incident. Never again would the Confederacy come as close to attaining European help for their cause. By this action Seward rewarded Lincoln's decision to include him in the cabinet by preventing a European war that the United States was unprepared to fight.

Secure in his role in Lincoln's cabinet, Seward acquired a new home close to the White House, which Lincoln visited regularly. While the White House was always a swarm of activity, Lincoln was able to find sanctuary by Seward's fireplace. As their relationship grew, the two men began holding conferences on a daily basis. It was during these after-hour conversations that Seward was able to convince Lincoln to hold back the announcement of the Emancipation Proclamation until after a military victory, lest it be heard as the "last shriek" of a failed administration. Seward continued as secretary of state after Lincoln's assassination.

Serving under President Andrew Johnson, Seward helped secure the passage of the Thirteenth Amendment outlawing slavery and went on to make the controversial decision to purchase Alaska in 1867. Today, Seward is still considered one of this country's best secretaries of state.

John C. Breckinridge: Too Little Too Late

In 1856, at the age of 36, John Breckinridge became the youngest vice president in U.S. history. Prior to that, Breckinridge had served in the Kentucky legislature and in the House of Representatives. In the 1850s he played a key role in the repeal of the Missouri Compromise and in securing passage of the Kansas-Nebraska Act. Breckinridge also ran for president in 1860, representing the southern wing of the Democratic party. Fearing that a divided party would give the Republicans the presidency, he offered to withdraw from the race if Stephen Douglas withdrew as well. Douglas declined the offer and split the Democratic vote with Breckinridge, who carried every state in the Deep South and earned 72 electoral votes, second only to the victorious Lincoln. While not a radical, Breckinridge believed in the constitutional protection of slavery and in the right of secession. When Kentucky declared for the Union in September 1861, and sought to arrest Breckinridge as a traitor, he joined the Confederate army as a brigadier general.

General Breckinridge earned a stellar reputation during the war and led troops at Bowling Green, Shiloh, Baton Rouge, Stones River, Vicksburg, Chickamauga, and Missionary Ridge, before being called upon by President Davis to serve in the thankless task as his secretary of war. Having served as one of the ablest secretaries the Federal War Department ever had before the war, President Davis kept a tight reign on all those who served in that capacity under his leadership. The inexperienced Leroy Walker, Davis's first secretary of war, was considered a mistake almost from

General John Breckinridge served as the last Confederate secretary of war. (Library of Congress)

the very start. After Walker resigned, Davis acted as his own secretary of war and appointed a series of men who had to content themselves with the administrative tasks of the office until, one by one, they resigned in frustration. When the Confederate military fortunes fell to their lowest point in early 1865, Davis finally appointed a secretary of war with actual military experience—John C. Breckinridge.

The change was almost immediate. Breckinridge's first act was to fire the inept Confederate commissary general. For four long years, Lucius B. Northrup, a good friend of President Davis, had displayed an almost criminal incompetence—the result being plenty of hungry and ragged Confederate soldiers. Breckinridge worked to revamp the Commissary Department, and within three weeks, General Robert E. Lee declared that his army had not been so well supplied in months. Breckinridge also took over the task of assigning officers to command and of recommending general officers for promotion—tasks that Davis had previously determined were exclusively his. In addition, Breckinridge organized the evacuation of Richmond and worked closely with General Lee to organize an escape route from the city. Once this was accomplished, Breckinridge managed the journey of the Confederate cabinet on its flight through North and South Carolina and into Georgia. It was during this period that Breckinridge provided his most important service for the Confederacy. At a time when President Davis was intent on continuing the war, even if it meant retreating west of the Mississippi River, Breckinridge counseled the president that it would be best to surrender. "The Confederacy should not be captured in fragments…, we should not disband like banditti, but…should surrender as a government, and…thus maintain the dignity of our cause." Breckinridge took part in the Sherman-Johnston surrender negotiations and personally put the document in Davis's hands. When Davis still resisted, Breckinridge insisted that "prompt steps be taken to put an end to the war." While Breckinridge came to the job of secretary of war too late to change the outcome, he succeeded in managing the defeat "in a manner that lent stature to the cause." After the war, General Lee acknowledged that Breckinridge was the "ablest of the war secretaries." Said Lee, "I was acquainted with him as…one of our Generals, but I did not know him till he was Secretary of War, and he [was] a lofty, pure strong man."

Edwin Stanton: Aspiring to the Supreme Court

There was no man in Washington who worked as hard or was as ambitious as Edwin Stanton. As soon as he moved to the capital in 1856, he began scheming to be appointed to an important role in the government and eventually, he hoped, an appointment on the Supreme Court. As a young man Stanton was an ardent abolitionist, yet he served as a delegate for the Democratic party in 1840 and campaigned for Martin Van Buren in 1844. He protested against the annexation of Texas, yet he favored the expansionist policies of James Polk in 1846. He joined the Free Soil party in 1848, which opposed the extension of slavery, and then switched to James Buchanan's pro-slavery wing of the Democratic party in 1856 and even served as Buchanan's attorney general in 1860. Yet, even as he was serving Buchanan, Stanton was forging ties with William Seward and other prominent Republicans. However, all of Stanton's planning seemed to go for naught when President Lincoln failed to appoint him to an important position in his administration. Overnight, Stanton became one of Lincoln's harshest critics and habitually referred to him as the "original gorilla." Even as he was criticizing Lincoln, Stanton began work currying favor with General-in-Chief George McClellan. In fact, Stanton's schemes were so tangled that when he finally secured the appointment as Lincoln's secretary of war in January 1862, three of Lincoln's top advisors, Salmon Chase, William Seward, and even the deposed Simon Cameron, took the credit.

While it is difficult to determine who was responsible for the choice, President Lincoln had no illusions about the type of man he was getting. Despite Stanton's prior insults, Lincoln felt that he could be of value to the government. Stanton's first act, not surprisingly, was to bar his erstwhile "friend," General McClellan, from the War Department. Said Stanton, "I will force this man to fight…. The champagne and oysters on the Potomac must be stopped." Stanton immediately focused his attention on the myriad of shady contractors who had secured contracts with the War Department under the previous secretary of war. Employing ruthless efficiency, Stanton proved Lincoln right by shutting down dozens of corrupt contractors and returning some semblance of honesty to the bidding

Edwin Stanton replaced Simon Cameron as secretary of war in 1862. (National Archives)

process. Stanton also returned to his abolitionist roots during his tenure as secretary of war. When Lincoln introduced the Emancipation Proclamation, Stanton was one of only two cabinet members who embraced it immediately. Stanton even issued a report that graphically illustrated the benefits of such a policy. Stanton argued that newly freed slaves could be put to work providing supplies for the Union army. "By striking down this system of compulsory labor which enables the leaders of the rebellion to control the resources of the people, the rebellion would die of itself." Throughout the rest of the war Stanton worked tirelessly to promote generals who would follow the policies set by Lincoln, while simultaneously weeding out those generals who would not.

Stanton remained secretary of war during Andrew Johnson's administration, but repeatedly butted heads with the new president over Reconstruction. By the midterm elections in 1866, Johnson had allied himself firmly with the conservative Democrats while Stanton had become a staunch advocate of the radical Republicans in Congress. At issue was Johnson's determination to carry out a lenient Reconstruction and to restore legal status to the Southern states as quickly as possible. The radical Republicans however, were equally determined to punish the South for the war and to implement and protect the rights granted in the Thirteenth and Fourteenth Amendments. In 1867, Congress passed the Tenure of Office Act, which forbade Johnson from removing members of his cabinet without consent from the Senate. Johnson defied the Act by dismissing Stanton who he felt was undermining his policies. Stanton reacted by barricading himself in the War Department while impeachment charges were brought against Johnson. The impeachment failed to pass by one vote, and Stanton ultimately resigned his position and returned to private life. He was rewarded for his loyal service when Ulysses Grant was elected president. Sadly, just four days after being nominated by Grant to the Supreme Court—his life-long ambition—Stanton died quietly at his home.

Judah Benjamin: Friend to the President

Born in the West Indies, Judah Benjamin was part of a surprisingly cosmopolitan cabinet, which included three foreign-born members, put together by Jefferson Davis in 1861. Benjamin remained in the cabinet throughout the war, one of only three members to survive the 17 changes made by Davis. Benjamin grew up in Charleston, South Carolina, attended school at Yale, and went on to study law and open a practice in Louisiana. He made a name for himself during the "Creole Case" in which slaves bound for New Orleans took over the brig *Creole* and sailed it to the British West Indies. An international incident erupted when Britain set free the slaves not involved in the mutiny. Benjamin wrote the brief for the case, which resulted in a criminal extradition treaty and a British promise to avoid "officious interference" with American ships. An Anglo-American commission eventually ruled in favor of the United States and rewarded the slave owners $110,330 in damages for the lost slaves.

Benjamin was elected to the United States Senate as a Whig in 1852 and as a Democrat in 1856, before resigning when Louisiana seceded in 1861. As one of his few friends, Davis wanted him in the cabinet, but due to Louisiana's small delegation, could only offer him the relatively insignificant position of attorney general. Benjamin drew criticism almost immediately for appearing "useless and lazy," and many found his somewhat effeminate nature suspicious. Thomas Cobb even implied that Benjamin's wife had been unfaithful because she bore a child even though Benjamin, in Cobb's words, was a "eunuch." John Wise said Benjamin had "more brains and less heart" than any other civic leader in the Confederacy. However, Benjamin had the one thing that trumped all these complaints—President Davis's friendship.

On the infrequent occasions that President Davis let his guard down, he admitted that the one thing he missed most was "time to enjoy social intercourse." In fact, other than Benjamin, Davis had very few friends. These included General Theophilus Holmes, General Thomas Hindman, General Braxton Bragg, and Commissary General Lucius Northrop. When Secretary of War Lucius P. Walker resigned his post to join the war, Davis took the opportunity to appoint Benjamin in his place. The rotund, ever-smiling Benjamin had no qualms about filling this post, despite his lack of military experience, and used his stinging pen to rebuke generals who fell into disfavor with Davis. Benjamin survived the scandal that almost resulted in the resignation of Stonewall Jackson but could not be saved after the disastrous loss of Roanoke Island in February 1862. The main complaint against Benjamin was that he did not supply the island defenders with an adequate supply of powder for their guns. The ever-loyal

Judah Benjamin served his friend Jefferson Davis in a variety of cabinet positions in the Confederate government. (National Archives)

Benjamin took the criticism in stride and never responded to the condemnation by explaining that there wasn't any powder to send. Gratified by Benjamin's loyalty, Davis switched him to the vacant position of secretary of state rather than lose his services altogether.

In his new role, Benjamin worked vigorously to secure European recognition for the Confederacy. He tried to convince the Pope to help curtail the vast numbers of Irish and German Catholics from emigrating to the United States and joining the Union army. He also sent ambassadors to a variety of European countries, hoping to secure foreign soldiers for the Confederacy. Much like Lincoln's secretary, William Seward, Benjamin took on many extra tasks and generally worked to make himself indispensable. Benjamin also supervised the Confederate Secret Service agents in Canada and had a hand in various schemes, which included infecting northern cities with small pox, the burning of New York City, interfering with the 1864 elections, setting up a Northwest Confederacy, and robbing banks in Vermont. There were, in all probability, other plots that have been lost to history because Benjamin destroyed all his personal and official papers at the end of the war. Fearing arrest and retribution, Benjamin fled to England after the war.

After securing a special ruling, Benjamin was admitted to the bar, opened a highly successful and lucrative law practice, and was named to the prestigious Queen's Counsel in 1869. Unlike almost all of his compatriots, Benjamin never revisited the Civil War in memoirs or articles. According to one friend, Benjamin did not live in the past: "He adopted England as his home and all but severed connections to his Confederate past."

Salmon Chase: Old Greenbacks

Throughout his adult life, Salmon Chase was guided by three underlying principles: The first was an unwavering belief that slavery should be abolished. The second was a strong religious conviction that bordered on the dogmatic. And the third was an unwavering appetite for political office. These tenets served Chase well in his political career, and he succeeded in being elected to the Senate in 1849 and then as Governor of Ohio, in 1855. After serving two terms, Chase rejoined the Senate in 1860 and was a strong rival of Abraham Lincoln's for the presidency before becoming Lincoln's secretary of the treasury. In the process, Chase never let party labels or affiliation get in the way of his steady progress, switching political parties nine times before ending up as an ardent abolitionist Republican in 1860. Along the way, Chase was, at one time or another, a member of the Abolition party, the Free Soil party, the American (or Know Nothing) party, the Republican party, and the Liberty party.

Chase's performance during his term of office was nothing short of remarkable. While others got to "fight" the war, Chase had to find ways to pay for it. During the initial phase of the war, Chase relied on short-term bank loans to raise money. Leaning heavily on financier Jay Cooke, Chase pioneered the idea of selling long-term bonds to ordinary people. The idea was a great success, and by the end of the war the Federal government had garnered $1.2 billion by selling these bonds. Other financial innovations implemented during Chase's tenure included the first federal income tax, the creation of the Bureau of Internal Revenue Service, the National Banking Act, and the Legal Tender Act. By the time Chase was finished, the entire monetary

Salmon Chase, "Old Greenbacks," served as President Lincoln's secretary of the treasury. (National Archives)

structure of the country had been dramatically altered by the dominance of paper currency, called "greenbacks," which were considered legal tender and used exclusively in the new national banking system.

Chase was a very active member of Lincoln's cabinet early in the war and pushed Lincoln to take a stronger stand against slavery. However, Chase wore out his welcome in the White House when his desire to challenge Lincoln in the 1864 presidential election became evident. At first Lincoln humored his treasury secretary, believing that Chase's service was too valuable to lose over his almost quixotic fixation with the presidency. Said Lincoln, "I have decided to shut my eyes, as far as possible, to everything of the sort. Mr. Chase makes a good Secretary and I shall keep him where he is." Lincoln described Chase's fixation as a "mild form of insanity," but he could not continue ignoring Chase's actions after several inflammatory pamphlets were published at his behest. The most famous, known as the Pomeroy Circular, insisted that Lincoln should step down for the good of the war effort and Chase should replace him. Chase's efforts backfired almost immediately and resulted in a surge of support for Lincoln. Chase offered his resignation—something he had done several times before—but Lincoln refused to accept it. However, once Lincoln was officially nominated at the party convention in Baltimore, Chase's days as a member of the cabinet were numbered. The next time Lincoln and Chase butted heads, this time over the disbursement of patronage in the Treasury Department, Chase once again submitted his resignation. Much to Chase's surprise and dismay, this time Lincoln accepted it.

This episode did not end Chase's public career. When Chief Justice Roger Taney died in October 1864, Lincoln nominated Chase for the position. Despite the unique demands of being the Chief Justice of the Supreme Court during the tumultuous postwar era, Chase still yearned to be president. When the Republicans nominated war hero Ulysses S. Grant in 1868, Chase openly solicited the Democratic nomination but, during the party's convention, lost out to New York ex-governor Horatio Seymour. The incongruity of Chase's earlier position as one of the nation's most radical abolitionist could not be reconciled with the Democratic platform allowing the Southern states to decide whether to grant suffrage to freed slaves. Even when Chase was on his deathbed, he was lobbying for the presidential nomination of the Liberal Party. This time Chase lost out to Horace Greeley, who went on to lose in the general election to Grant. The presidential grub, as Lincoln noted early in his presidency, had embedded itself deeply in Chase and never let go.

Simon Cameron and
Alexander Stephens: The Thorns

While men like Seward, Breckinridge, Stanton, Benjamin, and Chase made significant contributions to their respective presidents, there were cabinet members whose contributions can only be classified as questionable. Some, such as the Confederate secretary of war, Leroy P. Walker, realized that they were out of their depth and quickly resigned. President Lincoln was not so lucky with his secretary of war, Simon Cameron, whose idea of an honest politician was "one who will stay bought." Dubbed the "Winnebago Chief" for his dishonest dealings with Native American tribes, Cameron brought a strong delegation to the 1860 Republican convention and was rewarded with the promise of a cabinet seat in exchange for his support. When Lincoln learned of the deal, he withdrew the offer but eventually made Cameron his secretary of war to preserve peace within the party. Cameron quickly took advantage of the war effort by awarding large numbers of lucrative contracts to firms in his home state of Pennsylvania. He also routed the most profitable military traffic over railroads in which he held direct financial interests. Things got so bad that Congress created an investigative committee that condemned Cameron's activities. By January 1862, Lincoln had seen enough and sent Cameron to St. Petersburg as the U.S. Minister to Russia.

Simon Cameron, the "Winnabago Chief," was President Lincoln's first secretary of war. (Library of Congress)

There was one cabinet member who served as a presidential thorn throughout the war. Unfortunately for President Jefferson Davis, that man was his own vice president, Alexander Stephens. In what became known as the Cornerstone Speech, which he made in Savannah, Georgia, in 1861, Alexander Stephens made a vigorous defense of slavery: "Our new government is founded upon...the great truth, that the negro is not equal to the white man; that slavery—subordination to the superior race—is his natural and normal condition." However, Stephens came to oppose Davis on almost every other important issue, especially universal conscription and the suspension of habeas corpus. Things got so bad that Stephens, who referred to President Davis as his "poor old blind and deaf dog," left Richmond for his home in Georgia and joined ex-General Robert Toombs and Governor Joe Brown in calling for the removal of Davis and the opening of direct negotiations with Washington for the ending of the war. To the end, Stephens believed that the principles of state's rights should be upheld even if it meant losing the war. He codified this with the maxim: "Times change and men often change with them, but principles never!"

CHAPTER **3**

GLOBAL ASPECTS OF THE CIVIL WAR

The Confederacy's Only Foreign War

When the Confederacy was initially formed, one of its most difficult tasks was to build a navy that could hold its own against the Union navy. The strategy initiated by Secretary of the Navy Stephen Mallory was threefold. First, the Confederacy granted letters of marque and reprisal to small privately owned vessels (privateers) that could bring in needed supplies by running the Union naval blockade and by attacking unarmed merchant vessels. In the early stages of the war, this strategy was extremely successful, but running the blockade became more and more difficult as the war dragged on. Not only did the Union navy grow exponentially, from an initial 42-vessel fleet to the 671 ships employed at the end of the war, but the Confederacy also lost control of many of its vital port cities. Mallory also started constructing powerful ironclads, which had been used successfully by the British and French navies in the Crimean War. Again, the results were mixed. The CSS *Virginia* caused much consternation when it was initially launched, but the Union monitor class gunboats quickly regained control of the seas for the Union. Of the 50 or so Rebel ironclads that went into production, only two dozen were ever completed. Of these, only a handful participated in successful engagements before being overwhelmed by the much larger Union ocean and river fleets.

Secretary Mallory knew he needed more ships than the poorly equipped Confederate naval yards could ever hope to construct in order to match the production capabilities of the industrialized North. To even the odds, he turned to Europe. Mallory sent James Bulloch to England with orders to obtain fast-moving steam cruisers that could be converted into warships. Bulloch managed to procure

43

several such vessels before the program was shut down by Union agents working for Secretary of State Seward. Of these, the CSS *Florida* and the CSS *Alabama* were the most successful. Together, they captured or sank more than 100 Union merchant ships. (After the war, the United States was awarded $15.5 million from England, by an international tribunal, as compensation for Confederate ships that were constructed in British naval yards.)

In March 1863, a 1,150-ton iron screw steam cruiser built in Dumbarton, Scotland, was secretly purchased by the Confederate government and converted into a warship. Dubbed the CSS *Georgia* and commanded by Lieutenant William Maury, the Confederacy's newest cruiser immediately set sail in search of prizes in the South Atlantic. The CSS *Georgia* lacked the speed and luck of the more successful Confederate cruisers and was only able to capture nine prizes before her iron hull "became befouled by marine growth" and she was ordered to rendezvous off the coast of Morocco to transfer her guns to the CSS *Rappahannock*. Even though the CSS *Georgia*, now commanded by Lieutenant Evans, waited for several weeks, the CSS *Rappahannock* never appeared. (A machinery breakdown forced her to put into Calais, France, for repairs, and she was detained there for the duration of the war.) The only people the Rebel mariners saw during this time were a few native fishermen who traded fresh fish for small bits of scrap metal. Convinced that the locals were friendly, Lieutenant Evans allowed his men to go ashore for a little exercise and relaxation. Almost as soon as they reached the shore, the unarmed sailors were attacked by natives armed with spears and old-fashioned guns. After being roughed up, the shore party was escorted back to its boats and forced to return to the ship. Although the sailors were "disposed to treat [the] experience...as a good joke," Lieutenant Evans had different ideas. Being new to command, Evans ordered the ship to beat to quarters and gave orders to fire the ship's guns at the natives; "the guns roared and the screeching shells sped away to burst over the heads of the astounded Moors, who stood not upon the order of their going, but disappeared."

Confederate cruiser CSS Georgia *captured nine prizes before encountering natives along the shores of Morocco. (Naval Official Records)*

However, that did not end the engagement. The next day a fierce storm struck the coast and the CSS *Georgia* began to drag her anchor and drift toward the land. The natives appeared again and began to dance on the shore hoping that the CSS *Georgia* would be beached and the crew stranded. The engineer got the steam engine going, but two of its wooden cogs broke. For several hours the Confederate ship drifted closer and closer to the angry natives on the shore, before repairs could be made and the CSS *Georgia* was able to steam away. In the words of James Morgan, a sailor aboard the ship, thus ended "the Confederacy's only foreign war." The CSS *Georgia* eventually made her way back to France where she was decommissioned and sold out of service. After the war she became a Canadian merchant steamer and, in 1875, wrecked off the coast of Maine.

Mexico, Part One: Stillbirth of an Empire

While most of the Confederacy's diplomatic efforts were focused on England and France, President Jefferson Davis also had hopes of expanding the Confederacy's western borders. In 1861, after its war with the United States, Mexico was in a state of chaos and President Benito Juarez had only a small army in Mexico City at his command. The states in northern Mexico (Nuevo Leon, Chihuahua, Sonora, and Baja California) were, in the eyes of Davis, ripe for the plucking. At first, he attempted to negotiate directly with President Juarez. However, John Pickett, the Confederate ambassador sent to Mexico City, blundered badly by threatening a Confederate invasion and Juarez had him thrown in jail.

Shortly after Pickett was arrested, Governor Santiago Vidaurri of Nuevo Leon sent a letter to President Davis offering to annex his provinces to the Confederacy in return for a regiment of troops and enough artillery to protect his territory. Davis considered Vidaurri's offer "imprudent" and declined to accept it until similar agreements had been secured with other Mexican provincial leaders. Colonel James Reily, a Texas lawyer, was sent to negotiate with Governor Luis

Mexican President Benito Juarez lost power to the French-backed Archduke Maximillian in 1864. (Library of Congress)

Terrazas of Chihuahua and Governor Don Ignacio Pesqueira of Sonora. Despite optimistic reports returned by Reily, he was unable to secure any sort of agreement with the two Mexican governors. Eventually General George Wright, the Union commander of the Department of the Pacific, learned of Reily's activities. Wright dispatched a gunboat to the region with a letter warning that he had an army of 10,000 men "ready to pass the frontier." Governor Pesqueira ended the Confederate hopes of a Mexican empire by promising Wright that if any Confederates set foot in Mexico, he would "exterminate" them.

Mexico, Part Two: Napoleon in the New World

Jefferson Davis wasn't the only "foreign" leader to have an interest in Mexico. Emperor Napoleon III of France had dreams of creating an overseas empire. When Mexico defaulted on loans granted to President Juarez in 1861, England, France, and Spain decided to take matters into their own hands. Together, a joint expedition set sail for Veracruz in 1862 to seize the Customs House in an effort to collect the $80 million owed by the Mexican government. Soon after arriving, the British and Spanish troops, having collected what they could, departed. However, General Charles Latrille Laurency remained with an army of French troops and orders from Napoleon III to march on Mexico City. If successful, Laurency also had permission to continue his march into Texas and join Confederate forces stationed there. Confident that his veteran army would have no difficulties, Laurency was surprised by the stubborn defense put up by General Ignacio Zaragoza de Seguin's small ragtag army at Puebla. After two hours of hard fighting, the French army had expended most of its ammunition and a strong Mexican counterattack forced Laurency to withdraw in defeat. However, the Cinco de Mayo victory was only temporary. Napoleon III sent 30,000 reinforcements a year later, and the French easily took control of the country.

In 1864, Napoleon III convinced the unemployed Archduke Maximillian of Austria to accept the crown of Mexico. Prior to accepting the crown, the 30-year-old Maximillian had been the governor-general of Lombardy until that kingdom had been ceded to King Victor Emanuel II of Sardinia. Although Napoleon III's efforts in Mexico were a direct violation of the Monroe Doctrine, the hands of President Lincoln and Secretary of State Seward were tied by the necessity of keeping France out of the Civil War. The pragmatic Seward asked, "Why should we gasconade about Mexico when we are in a struggle for our own life?" Maximillian's reign in Mexico was doomed when the Civil War ended, however. Freed from the constraints of fighting the Confederacy, the United States sent 50,000 troops, commanded by General Phil Sheridan, to the Mexican border, and Secretary Seward filed a formal protest against the occupation. Faced with growing unrest in Mexico and the threats from the United States, Napoleon III withdrew the French troops leaving Maximillian to fend for himself. Maximillian was quickly captured by troops loyal to deposed President Juarez and executed on June 19, 1867.

Japan, Part One: War in the Pacific

On July 8, 1853, Commodore Matthew Perry sailed into Yedo (Tokyo) Bay with four warships and coerced the Tokugawa government into signing the Treaty of Kanagawa, which granted the United States diplomatic relations with Japan and secured trading rights in two Japanese ports (Hakodate and Shimoda). The treaty also granted the right of extraterritoriality, which meant United States diplomats were allowed to live in Japan but were subject to the laws of the United States. The first U.S. envoy arrived at Shimoda in August 1856 and signed a commercial treaty with Shogun Iesada. While Shogun Iesada favored opening Japan to foreign trade, many feudal lords were adamantly opposed to the

Lithograph published by Sarony & Co. depicting Commodore Perry during his first visit to Shui, Lew Chew, Japan, in 1853. (Library of Congress)

presence and growing influence of the gaijins (foreigners or non-Japanese). In 1863, violence broke out when the U.S. consulate was burned to the ground and Consul Robert Pruyn was forced to flee to Yokohama. To make matters worse, the Japanese Mikado announced that all "foreign devils" were to be expelled by June 25, 1863. That night, an American merchant ship bound for Nagasaki was attacked in a narrow channel called the Strait of Shimonoseki, between the islands of Kyushu and Honshu.

Fortunately for Consul Pruyn, the USS *Wyoming*, commanded by David McDougal, had just arrived off the coast of Japan on a mission to patrol the Pacific Ocean in search of the cruiser CSS *Alabama*. After conferring with Pruyn, McDougal steamed to the Shimonoseki Strait to deal with the offending ships. The Honshu side of the strait was controlled by Prince Choshiu—one of the most active of the anti-foreigner lords—and fortified by six shore batteries and three armed warships. Ignoring considerable fire from the shore batteries, McDougal focused on the Japanese ships. The USS *Wyoming* passed so close to one of these ships that her guns "seemed almost to touch the muzzles of the enemy." Despite being hit 20 times, the USS *Wyoming* managed to sink or disable all three enemy vessels and disable the shore batteries in just over an hour of hard fighting, at a cost of only five killed and seven wounded men. What made USS *Wyoming's* victory even more impressive was that the crew had never seen action before. According to Theodore Roosevelt, "had the action taken place at any other time than during the Civil War, its fame would have echoed all over the world."

Japan, Part Two: Back to Shimonoseki

McDougal's victory did not end the efforts of Prince Choshiu to close the Shimonoseki Strait to foreign merchant ships. Shortly after the USS *Wyoming* steamed back to America, the shore batteries were rebuilt and strengthened. Consul Pruyn summed up the situation this way: "Now that the ports are opened, the past and the present stand face to face.... One or the other must disappear. They cannot quietly coexist when brought into contact." Accordingly, Pruyn and the British minister, Sir Rutherford Alcock, drew up a plan which would drive the hostile Japanese away. On May 30, 1864, representatives from the United States, England, France, and Holland signed an agreement to take part in the joint operation against Choshiu's forces at Shimonoseki. After months of planning, a fleet of nine British, four Dutch, and three French warships gathered for the attack. Because there were no American ships available, a local steamer, the *Tai-Kiang,* was chartered to carry the American flag during the operation. The *Tai-Kiang,* armed with a 30-pound Parrott rifle, carried a British landing party and managed to get off 17 shots before the Japanese forces were overwhelmed.

The resulting treaty guaranteed that all ships passing through the Shimonoseki Strait would to be "treated in a friendly manner" and that all ships would be allowed to purchase "coal, provisions, wood, and water." The Japanese promised that no new forts would be built and no repairs would be made on the old ones. Finally, the government in Yedo (Tokyo) agreed to pay a "ransom," which included all the expenses of the expedition. Thus, even while the United States was engaged in fighting a civil war, it was beginning to play a large role in international events. Consul Pruyn was confident in his subsequent report to Washington that the expedition greatly contributed to, "if it has not secured altogether, our safety in Japan." For Japan, the expedition was the beginning of the end of the Tokugawa shogunate era. Shogun Iemochi died in 1866, and his successor was the last of his line to rule Japan, ending a 283-year reign. On July 4, 1868, Emperor Mutsuhito defeated the last of the Tokugawa forces and began a new era in which Japan would develop into a modern industrial and military power that could compete on equal standing with Europe and the United States.

Russia: A Gesture of Goodwill

While the monarchs of England and France secretly delighted in the American Civil War and the potential downfall of the world's first constitutional democracy, there was one European power that gave the Federal government in Washington unequivocal support from the very beginning. That country was Russia. Although Czar Alexander II freed the serfs in his country in 1861, Russian support derived more from its opposition to England and France, which had together defeated Russia in the Crimean War in 1856, than the Czar's love of democracy. Still, President Lincoln had Czar Alexander's letter of support, delivered by the Baron de Stoeckl in August 1861, sent to newspapers throughout the world. According to the

Czar, both nations were in an "ascending period of their development" and formed "a natural community of interests and of sympathy." At least one newspaper, the *New York Times*, pointed out the irony of Russia, an absolute monarchy, being the only European nation to "openly address a letter of sympathy to a Constitutional Government in its hour of trial."

Russian sailors photographed during their visit to New York City in 1863. (Library of Congress)

The growing friendship between Russia and the United States began to yield fruit when, in the fall of 1863, Russian fleets arrived in New York City and San Francisco. Russian Minister Baron Van Stoeckl announced that the visit was intended as a goodwill gesture, to show the world that Russia was lending support to the liberal government of the United States. A magnificent reception was held in New York on October 1, 1863, complete with a parade down Broadway, and on November 5, 1863, a Russian Ball was held at the Academy of Music. The affair was so grand that *Harper's Weekly* published pages of detailed illustrations of the event, and the accompanying feast, prepared by Delmonico, featured "12,000 oysters, 1,200 game birds, 250 turkeys, 400 chickens, 1,000 pounds of tenderloin, and 3,500 bottles of wine." Admiral Popov, commander of the Russian fleet docked in San Francisco, even offered to protect the bay from marauding Confederate cruisers. Popov's offer so impressed Naval Secretary Gideon Welles that he wrote "God bless the Russians" in his diary.

It wasn't until 1914 that the real reason for the "goodwill" tour of the Russian fleet was revealed when an American historian named Frank Golder was allowed to examine the archives of the Russian Ministry of the Marine. Golder determined that the Russian fleet set sail to America in order to be in ice-free waters in case of war in Europe. In 1930, a Russian scholar published the evidence in full. According to his investigation, the fleets were sent to American waters "to put them in the most favorable position for the opening of warlike activities with maximum of energy and productivity against England and France." Relations between Russia and the United States remained friendly after the war. When Czar Alexander II decided to sell Alaska to help pay off his growing international debt, he contacted his old friends in America. In 1867, Secretary of State Seward agreed to buy the territory for $7.2 million, or about two cents per acre. "Seward's Folly" looked like a sweet deal for Russia—until the discovery of gold in the region in 1880.

Oddities: Poland and the Vatican

The Polish revolt of 1863 that prompted the Russian fleet to scurry for safe harbor in the United States also left thousands of Polish exiles scattered throughout Europe. Colonel Valery Sulakowski, a Polish leader who served in the Confederate army, proposed organizing the exiles to fight for the Confederacy in exchange for land grants. In August 1863, a delegation of Polish officers ran the blockade and arrived in Richmond, Virginia, to meet with President Davis. At the meeting,

Pope Pius IX considered granting official recognition to the Confederacy in 1863. (Library of Congress)

Davis agreed to send 50,000 English pounds to London to secure transportation for the exiles to Texas. Davis also prepared letters of introduction for the Polish soldiers who were to return to Europe to enlist the foreign recruits. However, the plan fell apart after a newspaper in Charleston announced that 30,000 Polish troops were expected to join the Confederate army very soon. Needless to say, no recruits ever arrived.

In addition to attempting to recruit European soldiers for the Confederate army, President Davis also tried to cut off the flow of Europeans to the Union army. Knowing that great numbers of Irish and German Catholics were being drawn to America and into the Union army by the large bounties being offered, Davis directed his attention to Pope Pius IX. Davis's representative, Dudley Mann, met with Cardinal Antonelli, the Papal State secretary, in November 1863.

Antonelli, an admirer of the Confederate military successes, told Mann that Davis's name "would rank with those of the most illustrious statesman of the time." When Mann informed Antonelli that the Union army would not be able to continue the war without the thousands of European Catholics that had joined the ranks, Antonelli arranged for a meeting with the Pope. The meeting progressed positively until the Pope brought up the issue of slavery. When asked if it would not be wise for the Confederacy to "consent to gradual emancipation," Mann tried to explain to the Pope the benefits of slavery. According to Mann, freedom would convert the "well-cared for civilized Negro into a semi-barbarian." Mann went on to explain that the poor Irish and German recruits were "invariably placed in the most exposed points on the battlefield," and that the North would have "broken down months ago" if not for their efforts. At the end of the 40-minute interview, the exultant Mann wrote a glowing report to Secretary of State Benjamin promising a letter from the Pope to Davis that the Confederacy could publish. However, Davis's hopes for papal intervention were dashed when the letter arrived on December 3, 1863. Instead of being pro-Confederate, the letter was disappointingly vague, saying only that he would pray for peace to be restored "upon all the people in America."

PART TWO

THE GENERALS

On September 1, 1864, the Confederate army, commanded by General John Bell Hood, evacuated the city of Atlanta. Hood's failure to hold Atlanta became one of the major turning points of the war. Throughout the war, only eight men—including Hood—held the rank of full general in the Confederate army. These men were appointed by President Davis to command the largest Confederate armies and to defend the most vital areas in the South. In many ways, the fortunes of the Confederacy were pinned to the successes and failures of these men. This section of the book will explore President Davis's strict adherence to the convention of seniority in the military and explain how this hampered his ability to provide quality leadership to some of the armies of the Confederacy. In addition, an assortment of military officers who, either through bad timing, bad judgment, or bad luck, spectacularly failed will be highlighted, as will the many elderly generals who, instead of enjoying their golden years, found themselves embroiled in civil war.

CHAPTER 4

THE BEST AND
THE WORST OF THE
SENIOR CITIZEN GENERALS

What Happened to the Old Guard

Thousands of people streamed to Washington on May 23 and 24 of 1865, for a glimpse of the victorious Union army parading in one last Grand Review. On the first day, 26-year-old General George Armstrong Custer stole the show after he "lost" control of his horse and charged past the reviewing stand twice. On the second day, they were thrilled by General William Tecumseh Sherman's 65,000 long-striding, weather-beaten "bummers." What they didn't see were any of the senior citizen generals who had commanded the U.S. Army when the war began. These men—all veterans of past wars who had come up through the ranks at a time when the army prized seniority above all else—were long gone, and their deeds were all but forgotten.

Yet before the war, these venerable generals held almost every high-ranking position in the U.S. Army. The average age of the four top-ranking line officers (Winfield Scott, David Twiggs, John Wool, and William Harney) was 70, and all but one of the heads of the eight army bureaus had been in active service since the War of 1812. The youngest member of the general staff was 53-year-old Quartermaster General Joseph E. Johnston, who took over for a man who had died after serving in that position for 44 years. Johnston served only briefly before resigning to join the Confederate army. The commander of the U.S. Army was 74-year-old Winfield Scott. While a true war hero, Scott was extremely overweight, suffered from dropsy, and tended to fall asleep in cabinet meetings.

Thousands attended the victorious Union army's march through Washington, in a Grand Review, in May 1865. (Library of Congress)

Winfield Scott: Old Fuss and Feathers

Winfield Scott joined the army in 1808 as a captain of the light artillery. He soon ran into trouble with his commanding officer and was suspended from service in 1810 after being court-martialed. After spending a year out of the service, Scott rejoined the army to fight in the War of 1812. In his first battle, Scott's small force was ambushed by a party of Mohawks during the invasion of Queenstown Heights. Scott was captured, and 270 of his 290 men were either killed or wounded. After spending four months as a prisoner, Scott redeemed himself by leading a successful assault against Fort George, on May 13, 1813. For his performance, Scott was promoted. He was wounded a year later at Lundy's Lane and was again promoted for bravery, as his men bore the brunt of the fighting in the second bloodiest battle of the war (and the bloodiest ever on Canadian soil).

After the War of 1812, Scott served a long and varied career. In 1832 he was sent to Charleston, South Carolina, to deal with the Nullification Crisis. He later supervised the expulsion of the Cherokee Indians from Georgia, which culminated in the Trail of Tears in 1838. He also helped to avert fighting on the Maine border in what came to be known as the Aroostook War. However, Scott's supreme battle-field victories occurred during the Mexican War. After invading and capturing

Vera Cruz, Scott led his army to victories at Cerro Gordo, Contreras, and Chapultepec before leading his victorious army into Mexico City. After the war— and by then a national hero—Scott was promoted to (brevet) lieutenant-general and touted as a potential future president. (He ran unsuccessfully for president, as a Whig, in 1852.)

The elderly General Scott did his best to rise to the challenge when civil war erupted. He devised a complicated plan for defeating the Confederacy that was predicated on blockading all the southern ports. Scott warned that "the great danger now pressing upon us [is] the impatience of our patriotic and loyal Union friends." Scott lost favor with President Lincoln when he opposed holding or even trying to resupply Fort Sumter, and his so-called "Anaconda Plan" was shelved in favor of a quick strike at the Confederate army at Manassas, Virginia. When this attack ended in disaster, Scott himself was shelved in favor of the much younger General George McClellan. Although General Winfield Scott was forced to retire on November 1, 1861, he lived long enough to see the Lincoln administration, after a long series of failures, return to implement the Anaconda Plan and ultimately win the war. After visiting the now retired Scott in 1862, Lincoln remarked, "I cannot but think we are still his debtors."

A Currier and Ives print of General Winfield Scott, who led American forces to victory in the Mexican War and became the highest-ranking officer in the U.S. Army. (Library of Congress)

David Twiggs: All I Have Is in the South

The second most senior general in the U.S. Army was 71-year-old David Twiggs, commander of the Department of Texas. Like Scott, Twiggs joined the army as a captain during the War of 1812. After returning to civilian life for 11 years, Twiggs rejoined the army and decided to make it a career. He was rewarded for his performance in the Black Hawk War by being promoted to colonel and given command of the newly created Second Regiment of Dragoons, which was sent to Florida to fight the Seminoles in 1836. It was there that Twiggs earned the nickname "the Bengal Tiger" and a reputation for being able to curse a man out of his boots. He also made a name for himself with his practice of taking the battle to the enemy rather than responding to Seminole attacks in one of the fiercest Native American wars in U.S. history. The Second Dragoons saw action next at the start of the Mexican War in 1846 at the battle of Palo Alto. For his part in the victory, Twiggs was promoted to brigadier general and given command of a division. At the battle of Cerro Gordo, Twiggs led the successful assault that carried the day. When asked how far to charge, he responded, "Charge them to hell." Twiggs won another brevet promotion after the battle of Monterery and was also awarded a sword with a jeweled hilt and a gold scabbard by a thankful U.S. Congress.

After the war Major General Twiggs was given command of the Department of the West, and he maintained his headquarters in St. Louis, Missouri. However, in December 1860, Secretary of War John B. Floyd transferred Twiggs to San Antonio to command the Department of Texas. Floyd's motives for sending the Georgian and confirmed Southern sympathizer to command in Texas (where 15 percent of the men in the army were stationed) were suspect at best, and Floyd soon resigned his position amid a flurry of allegations that he had sent money and arms south, in preparation for the impending war. (Floyd was rewarded for his "loyalty" by immediately being granted a commission as a general in the Confederate army.)

On December 13, 1860, Twiggs officially took over command of the Department of Texas from Colonel Robert E. Lee and was given explicit instructions to protect government property without waging war or taking aggressive action. Twiggs responded in a letter to General Scott in Washington: "I am placed in a most embarrassing situation. I am a southern man and…as soon as I know Georgia has separated from the Union I must…follow her…. All I have is in the South." In private, Twiggs was more revealing. "If an old woman with a broomstick should come…to demand the public property, I would give it to her." On February 15, 1860, he received notice that he was to be relieved of his command as soon as his successor, Colonel Waite, (only 65 miles away, at Camp Verde) reached San Antonio. However, before Waite arrived, a thousand armed Texans, commanded by Ben McCulloch, surrounded the Federal garrison. Despite having already been officially relieved of duty, Twiggs not only surrendered his small command of 165 men, he also negotiated the surrender of all military forces and stores in Texas. In all, Twiggs gave up $1.6 million in government

General David Twiggs, a hero during the Mexican War, gave Texas to the Confederacy in 1860. (Library of Congress)

property, 20 military installations, 44 cannons, 400 pistols, 1,900 muskets, 500 wagons, and 950 horses. In a span of only 67 days, Twiggs not only trashed his 48-year military career, he delivered the state of Texas to the Confederacy. Five days after he surrendered, the Texas Secession Convention passed an Ordinance of Secession. Widely suspected of treason, Twiggs was given a dishonorable discharge from the U.S. Army for "treachery to the flag." The Confederate army welcomed the disgraced Twiggs with open arms by giving him a commission as major general and assigning him to command Department Number 1 (which included Louisiana, southern Mississippi, and southern Alabama). However, suffering from failing health after his ordeal, Twiggs retired before assuming his full duties and died on July 15, 1862.

John Wool: Hero of Troy

It came as no surprise when John Wool decided on a military career. His father had served with "Mad" Anthony Wayne during the storming of Stony Point in the Revolutionary War, and his four uncles had participated in the invasion of Quebec and the battle of Bennington. Wool raised a company of volunteers from Troy, New York, and received a commission as captain in 1812. He led his men at the battle of Queenstown Heights and was severely wounded in both thighs. Promoted after the battle, Wool recovered sufficiently to participate in the battle of Plattsburg where he was again promoted for gallantry. After the war, in 1816, Colonel Wool was made inspector-general of the army, and he served in that capacity for the next 20 years, until being sent to Georgia to oversee the expulsion of the Cherokee from their homeland. There, Wool ran into trouble and was arrested because of his efforts to provide adequate food and clothing for the Native Americans. Although eventually cleared by a court of inquiry, Wool was replaced by Winfield Scott, who was more aggressive in carrying out this unpleasant duty.

Wool's organizational skills were put to the test when the United States geared up for war with Mexico in 1856. In less that six weeks, Wool had 12,000 armed and equipped men ready for the field. He then recruited and equipped 3,000 additional men for his own command and marched them overland 900 miles to reach General Taylor's army in time for the battle of Buena Vista. For the duration of the Mexican War, Wool served as Taylor's second-in-command. For his efforts, he was promoted after the war and given command of the Department of the East where, except for a brief period when he was sent to Oregon, he served until civil war broke out in 1861.

Only two years younger than his commanding general Winfield Scott, Wool suffered from some age-related physical infirmities (his hands trembled and he often repeated his orders), but unlike Scott, he was still relatively active and could still mount a horse. When the Civil War began, Wool rose to the challenge by organizing and equipping the first regiments New York sent to Washington. In the spring of 1861, he sent badly needed reinforcements to Colonel Dimmick at

General John Wool was sent home, at the age of 74, after his performance during the New York City Draft Riot. (Library of Congress)

Fortress Monroe, and his aggressive action prevented this Federal stronghold from being captured by the Confederates—a fate that befell most of the other Federal installations located in the South. Fortress Monroe was subsequently used by General McClellan as a base for his Peninsular Campaign in 1862. During McClellan's slow advance, Wool (then commanding the Department of Virginia) was extremely critical of McClellan's leisurely pace and took it upon himself to capture the Gosport Naval Yard at Norfolk, Virginia.

President Lincoln, who had been present during Wool's advance on Norfolk, thought this a fitting swan song for his active military career and, shortly afterwards, transferred Wool to a less strenuous command in New York City. However, when draft riots broke out in the city in July 1863, Wool found himself in the thick of the action once again. Although he had precious few troops to suppress the rioters, Wool managed to keep control over most of the city until reinforcements arrived. Just as he was penning a dispatch to Washington to report that he had regained control of the city, Wool received notice that he was relieved of command. Stunned, Wool could not believe his 51-year military career was ending so ignominiously. After returning to his home in Troy, Wool sent long letters to the War Department seeking exoneration for his peremptory dismissal, but to no avail. He continued to do so, in letters to President Grant, until he died in 1869. Although his long service to his country was largely forgotten, the city of Troy remembered their hometown hero by erecting a 75-foot monument in his honor after the war.

William Harney: Indian Fighter

At 61, Harney was the baby of the bunch, and the only line officer to have been born in the 19th century. He joined the army at 18 as a second lieutenant and spent his early years in the army chasing Jean Lafitte and other river pirates who infested the Gulf of Mexico. However, the fiery redhead made a name for himself fighting in the Seminole War. Enraged after his camp had been attacked and several of his men killed in their sleep, he led a punitive expedition through the tangled swamps of the Everglades to exact revenge. Harney succeeded in finding Chekika, the "Spanish Indian" chief who had led the attack, and he captured and hung all the warriors in the small band. For his success, Harney was promoted to colonel and given command of the Second Dragoons. During the Mexican War, Harney ran into trouble after defying the orders of General Scott and was court-martialed. After an apology, Harney was reinstated in time to perform brilliantly while leading attacks at El Telegrafo and La Ataberry. When the war ended, Harney was promoted to brigadier general for his role in the battle of Cerro Gordo.

Harney was ordered to the Great Plains in 1854 to lead an expedition against the Sioux in retaliation for the Grattan Massacre, where 30 troopers were killed while trying to obtain payment for a stolen cow. Using tactics he had perfected in Florida, Harney surrounded the Brule Sioux village of Chief Little Thunder, despite the fact that these villagers had had nothing to do with the previous year's battle. After approaching under a flag of truce, Harney refused Little Thunder's offer of surrender and ordered his men to attack. In what came to be known as the Ash Hollow Massacre, Harney's men killed 86 men, women, and children. Harney followed that up by marching to Fort Pierre, where he met with a large delegation of Sioux who agreed to never again molest travelers in the Platte Valley.

Harney was then given orders to lead an expedition to Salt Lake City to reestablish governmental control over the Mormons who had settled there. However, Harney was relieved before reaching Utah Territory after President Buchanan learned that he intended to hang the religious leader Brigham Young and his 12 advisors. Harney was then sent to command the Department of Oregon and almost immediately found himself embroiled in another controversy. At issue was the death of a pig on San Juan Island. The island was claimed by both England and the United States, and when an American settler killed a pig belonging to the Hudson's Bay Company, British authorities threatened to arrest the culprit. Harney responded by sending a small force under the command of Captain George Picket

General William Harney led American forces during the Ash Hollow Massacre. (Library of Congress)

to the island. The British retaliated by sending several warships and threatening military action. When President Buchanan learned of the crisis he was shocked that Harney had allowed the situation to escalate to such proportions over the actions of one angry farmer. Harney was recalled, and General Winfield Scott was sent to clean up the mess.

Harney's next assignment proved to be even more troubling. As the new commander of the Department of the West, Harney found himself squarely in the middle of Governor Claib Jackson's attempt to lead Missouri into the Confederacy. Lacking the political sophistication to deal with such a delicate situation, Harney at first played down the threat in his dispatches to Washington. When he finally realized how critical the situation was, he struck a deal with General Price, the commander of the Missouri state militia, promising not to make any military movements as long as Price was able to maintain order in the state. The so-called "Price-Harney" agreement greatly angered Congressman Francis Blair, who had been working hard to curb the influence of Price's pro-Southern militia. Blair convinced Secretary of War Cameron to relieve Harney and replace him with General Nathaniel Lyon, an ardent abolitionist. Harney's inglorious removal and recall was made even more humiliating when he was captured by Confederate forces en route to Washington. However, Harney's Southern roots were well-known, and he was quickly released. Harney waited for two years for another command before realizing that his services were no longer wanted. He officially retired from military service in 1863.

In addition to the four highest-ranking line officers, almost every other high-ranking officer in the U.S. Army in 1861 had been in active service since the War of 1812. The highest-ranking officer to resign and join the Confederate army was Samuel Cooper. A career staff officer, Cooper had served as adjutant and inspector general since 1838, and his last official act was to sign the order of dismissal from the army for General Twiggs. Cooper went on to serve in the same capacity, as the highest-ranking staff officer in the Confederate army for the duration of the war. The Union army also turned to a senior to command one of its main field armies at the start of the war. Irish-born Robert Patterson served in the Pennsylvania militia in the war of 1812 and again as a general of Pennsylvania volunteers in the Mexican War, before being tapped by General Scott to command the 14,000 man army at Harper's Ferry. Patterson was ordered to hold General Joe Johnston's smaller force in place near Winchester, Virginia, while the rest of the army advanced on Manassas. However, he failed miserably and Johnston slipped away in time to help the Confederacy win the first major battle of the war. For his efforts, the 69-year-old general was mustered out of military service on July 27, 1861.

James Ripley: Ripley Van Winkle

One senior citizen who did not get the opportunity to leave his mark during the Civil War was Colonel Henry K. Craig. This chief of the Ordnance Department was replaced on April 23, 1861, when it became apparent that he had allowed the department, which was responsible for providing weapons and ammunition to the swiftly growing Union army, to become disorganized and mired in red tape. James Ripley, a spry 67-year-old, was chosen to take his place and, by all accounts, did an admirable job restoring administrative order.

Ripley, another War of 1812 veteran, had served in the army since receiving his commission from West Point in 1813. He was assigned to the artillery until his transfer to the Ordnance Department in 1832. He spent the majority of his service prior to the war as superintendent of the United States' largest armory in Springfield, Massachusetts. Ripley's tenure at the Springfield Armory was checkered at best. One of his most controversial acts was when he shut down the facility for retooling and then required all workers to reapply for their old jobs when the facility reopened. Worker resentment grew so large that Ripley had to install an iron fence made from outdated artillery pieces to protect the installation after a string of vandalism and arson at the installation. Shortly after Ripley was hung in effigy from a flagpole, he was reassigned to the Ordnance Department in Washington.

In one sense, Ripley was an ideal candidate for heading the Ordnance Department. He had no problem rejecting the unending stream of new and improved weaponry that was offered to the War Department. One such invention was an exploding musket shell that was invented by Samuel Gardiner in 1862. Although some of these shells made their way to the Union army through outside purchases, Ripley was adamant that it had "no value as a service projectile." After the war, the United States and most other European nations agreed to outlaw the shell. Another example was the 2-pounder Woodruff gun. Although President Lincoln pushed for the small cannon's acceptance, Ripley successfully blocked its introduction into the Union arsenal. When a few privately purchased pieces made their way into the army, they were found to be useful only as a source of amusement. One cavalryman wrote: "They were of no value and were generally voted a nuisance. They were never known to hit anything, and never served any useful purpose, except in promoting cheerfulness in the regiment. The men never tired of making jokes…about them."

Ripley's distrust of new weapons included his insistence that repeating rifles were too expensive, too wasteful of ammunition, and too delicate for active service. Despite several tests that showed such weapons as the Henry rifle could fire more than a hundred shots in five minutes, consistently hit a small target more than 300 feet away, and could be fired in excess of a thousand times without cleaning, Ripley refused to order more than a token amount for service. Ripley also blocked the introduction of the breech-loading rifles into military service. Although he did agree that breech-loading carbines were fit for cavalry service, Ripley was steadfast in his conviction that the infantry should be equipped with the single-shot muzzle-loading Springfield rifle or its equivalent. Eventually, President Lincoln and Secretary of War Edwin Stanton grew impatient with Ripley's intolerance of the improved repeating rifles and breech-loaders and, in September 1863, he was forced to step aside. Ripley spent the rest of the war inspecting forts along the New England coast.

The negative impact Ripley had on the Union war effort cannot be overemphasized. Although he did possess good organizational skills and was successful in the difficult task of procuring enough weapons and ammunition for the swiftly growing Union army in the beginning of the war, his resistance to technological innovations deprived the Union army of gaining a significant advantage on the battlefield until the later stages of the war. When repeating rifles began to appear in significant quantities on the battlefield, one disgruntled Rebel soldier called them "the damnyankee rifles you load on Sunday and fire all week." No better example can be found of the impact these weapons might have had during the Civil War than to examine the battle of Koniggratz, the only battle in the Seven Weeks' War between Austria and Prussia in 1866. The Prussian army had adopted the Needle gun in 1841, which could fire five shots a minute, while the Austrians still relied on a single-shot Lorenz muzzle-loader. In the battle, the Prussians won an overwhelming victory and inflicted 43,000 casualties while suffering only 9,000 of its own. One can only imagine what such a weapon could have achieved in the hands of Union soldiers in 1861.

CHAPTER 5

THE TOP GENERALS OF THE CONFEDERACY

The Perils of Seniority

When the newly born Confederate States of America chose Jefferson Davis to be its inaugural president, they were getting a man with a solid military background. Davis graduated from West Point in 1828 and served with distinction as a lieutenant in the Black Hawk War in 1831 and as a colonel in the Mexican War in 1847. After resigning his military commission due to poor health, Davis represented the state of Mississippi as a congress-man and as a senator. In addition, he served as secretary of war during President Franklin Pierce's adminis-tration from 1852–1856. He would have dearly loved to serve the Confederacy in a military capacity and accepted the position of president only with great reluctance. Thus it should not be surprising that, in his capacity as commander-in-chief of the Confed-erate army, Davis respected and ad-hered to the most cherished military tradition in U.S. Army: seniority.

President Jefferson Davis, arriving on the field at Manassas, Virginia. (Library of Congress)

Abraham Lincoln, on the other hand, had very little formal military training prior to his election in 1860. Although Lincoln served briefly in the Black Hawk War and was elected captain of his militia company, he saw no combat. Recognizing his lack of experience, Lincoln was reticent to inject his own opinions into military matters. But he was much more willing than Jefferson Davis to give young officers high-ranking positions of authority in the military. As far as Lincoln was concerned, winning battles was far more important than matters of seniority. Lincoln did have an advantage in the respect that the Union army used a two-tier command system. The first tier was reserved for regular army promotions while the second tier was used only for officers commanding volunteer soldiers. In addition, the Union army still used and recognized brevet promotions. These were usually awarded for acts of valor. Although a brevet promotion was largely symbolic, it did allow the officer in question to serve at a higher rank although he would not receive the pay of that rank or accrue any seniority at the higher rank.

Before the war ended, nearly 1,400 Federal officers were rewarded with brevet promotions to the rank of either brigadier or major general. (There were so many brevet promotions at the end of the war that the entire system was abolished in 1869.) As a result, an officer could hold as many as four separate ranks at any one time. For example, George Armstrong Custer received numerous promotions during the war and, on June 29, 1863, was made a brigadier general in the U.S. Volunteers. At the same time, he was a brevet major in the regular army and also held a nominal rank of first lieutenant in the regular army. Custer received additional promotions during the war until he was a full major general of Volunteers and a brevet major general in the regular army. However, his permanent rank in the army was as a captain—a promotion he received on May 8, 1864. When the war ended he reverted to that rank. Due to this low rank, Custer had to scramble to remain in the much smaller peacetime army before eventually being promoted to lieutenant colonel in the Seventh Cavalry. It was in that rank that he commanded the ill-fated expedition that ended in disaster at Little Big Horn.

Although complicated, the system allowed Lincoln and his military advisors considerable leeway to promote younger officers without having to worry about seniority. A prime example occurred just a few days before Gettysburg when Custer, along with Captains Wesley Merritt and Elon Fansworth, was promoted to brigadier general (U.S. Volunteers) ahead of dozens of cavalry officers with more experience. In this case, the promotions of the "boy generals" to brigade command worked out well, as Merritt and Custer went on to have fine careers. Farnsworth was killed at Gettysburg only days after receiving his promotion.

The Confederate army only had one tier of rank—the Provisional Army of the Confederate States, or PACS. They did try to implement a separate organization for professional soldiers, but that never got past the planning stage. In addition, the Confederate army did not use brevet promotions. Thus, seniority became even more important in the Confederate army than it was in the prewar U.S. Army.

Seniority was definitely on the mind of Jefferson Davis on August 21, 1861 when he submitted the names of the five officers who would be given the rank of full general, the highest in the Confederate service. First on the list was Samuel Cooper, given the rank as of May 16, 1861; second was Albert Sidney Johnston, as of May 30, 1861; third was Robert E. Lee, as of June 14, 1861; fourth was Joseph E. Johnston, as of July 4, 1861; and the fifth general was P.G.T. Beauregard, as of July 21, 1861. The task of commanding the largest armies and defending the most important areas of the Confederacy would fall to these men. Almost as soon as the ink was dry on the paper, Joe Johnston began complaining that he should be the top-ranking general in the army. Johnston's argument was based on the fact that, due to his appointment as quartermaster general of the U.S. Army in 1860 and the accompanying promotion to brigadier general that went with it, he outranked the others. Davis countered that argument by pointing out that Johnston's rank was a staff rank and could not be compared to ranks held in field positions. Johnston felt that Davis's action was a violation of the letter of the law and wrote to Davis, detailing his objections. However, this was a dispute that Johnston was destined to lose.

Operating within this command structure, Davis kept Joe Johnston as commander of the army in Manassas, Virginia. Albert Sidney Johnston was given command of the Confederate forces in Tennessee, with P.G.T. Beauregard as his second-in-command. Robert E. Lee, after an unsuccessful stint as a field commander in western Virginia, returned to Richmond to serve as Davis's military advisor. The elderly Cooper retained his staff role as adjutant and inspector general of the army.

Later in the war another full general, Edmund Kirby Smith, was commissioned to command the Confederate forces west of the Mississippi River. After Albert Sidney Johnston was killed at Shiloh, Davis chose Braxton Bragg as his replacement, giving him a commission as a full general in the Confederate army. In addition, John Bell Hood was given a temporary commission as a full general when he was tapped to replace Joe Johnston as commander of the Army of Tennessee in 1864. That commission was revoked when Hood resigned after the disastrous defeats at Franklin and Nashville, Tennessee, late in 1864. In all, only eight men ever held the rank of full general in the Confederate army, and it was from these men who Jefferson Davis had to choose, for better or for worse, to fend off the relentless attacks of the Union army.

The First Crisis in Command:
Joe Johnston Is Wounded

The feud between Joe Johnston and President Davis, which began with Johnston's unhappiness over his rank, escalated throughout the fall and winter of 1861–1862, when Johnston, feeling that it was unnecessary and hazardous, hesitated to implement Davis's directive to brigade all troops from the same state together. Then, in early spring, Johnston withdrew without permission from his exposed position near Manassas, which necessitated the destruction of large amounts of food and supplies that could not be taken along. Finally, Johnston—

again without notifying Davis—withdrew from Yorktown, Virginia, several months later without a fight and kept retreating until the Union army, commanded by George McClellan, was within 12 miles of the Confederate capital.

Under increasing pressure from President Davis, Johnston announced that he had a plan to attack the Federal army. Davis rode out to observe the attack, only to discover that it had been delayed and General Johnston had neglected to inform him. Finally, on May 31, 1862, Johnston was ready, and the long-awaited attack finally began. However, Johnston's well-calibrated plan quickly fell apart, and the battle (Seven Pines) disintegrated into an uncoordinated series of thrusts and counterthrusts.

General Joe Johnston, one of the eight full generals in the Confederate army. (Library of Congress)

Just when it looked like Johnston's men would win the day, Union reinforcements, commanded by General "Bullhead" Sumner, arrived on the field to stem the advance. A frustrated Johnston, riding too close to the battlefield at the end the day, was seriously wounded when he was hit in the right shoulder by a bullet and in the chest by a shell fragment.

General Gustavus W. Smith took temporary command after Johnston's injury. The ex-street commissioner of New York City was the highest-ranking major general in the army, with a commission dated September 19, 1861. However, Smith was in failing health and not considered a serious candidate for the position. In fact, he suffered what amounted to a nervous breakdown following the battle and had to be relieved of command. (He eventually resigned from the Confederate army in January 1863, because so many junior officers were promoted over his head.) The obvious choice was Robert E. Lee, yet Lee had already disappointed Davis twice. The first time was when Lee had failed to retake western Virginia early in the war. The second time was when he was sent to inspect and improve the fortifications along the Atlantic seaboard. There were so many complaints about "Spades" Lee that Davis decided to recall him to Richmond.

Riding back to Richmond the night after the battle, Jefferson Davis wrestled with the decision. Who should be given command of the army charged with the defense of Richmond? There were few alternatives. Albert Sidney Johnston had been killed at Shiloh, and P.G.T. Beauregard, who had taken over for him, was now in of command the army in Corinth, Mississippi. Davis's riding companion, the 55-year-old General Lee, was the only full-ranking general available, and he could take command immediately. Before the two men arrived at Richmond, Davis had reached his decision. For better or for worse, the commander of the (soon to be named) Army of Northern Virginia was to be Robert Edward Lee. There was one person on the other side of the lines who applauded the elevation of Lee. According to General George McClellan, Lee was "too cautious and weak under grave responsibility." McClellan concluded that Lee was "likely to be timid and irresolute in action." This would be one of the many times that McClellan's judgment would turn out to be terribly wrong.

The Second Crisis in Command: P.G.T. Beauregard Goes AWOL

President Davis's decision to turn over the reins of the Army of Northern Virginia to General Lee went so well that he never had to make another command decision of that type in the East for the rest of the war. He was not so fortunate with his decisions regarding the commander of the Confederate army in the West. At the beginning of the war, Davis had no qualms about handing over command of the armies in Tennessee to Albert Sidney Johnston. In fact, Davis thought so highly of him that he devoted most of his attention to matters in Virginia, leaving the details of defending Tennessee to A.S. Johnston. This proved to be a mistake, after a series of stunning Union victories gave the Union control over most of Tennessee. A.S. Johnston regrouped his shattered command at Corinth, Mississippi, and prepared to launch a surprise attack at Shiloh that he hoped would change the fortunes of the war. Unfortunately, he was killed leading a cavalry charge, and command devolved to P.G.T. Beauregard. After the first day's assault failed to drive the Union army into the Tennessee River, Beauregard struggled to hold the army together on the second day of the battle, in the face of repeated Union attacks. Eventually, Beauregard safely withdrew his men to nearby Corinth, to await the inevitable Union advance.

General Pierre Gustave Toutant Beauregard had had almost as many difficulties dealing with President Davis as did Joe Johnston. After the battle of Manassas, Beauregard was sent to Tennessee, for the most part, to get him out of Davis's hair. When he got there, "Old Bory" was shocked to find out how weak the Confederate defenses were. After doing what he could to shore them up, Beauregard helped Albert Sidney Johnston rebuild the army and even drew up the battle plans for the Shiloh attack. After the battle, Beauregard used every trick available to slow the Union advance towards the critical railroad junction at Corinth. Finally, after almost two months of bluff and bluster, Beauregard conducted a secret retreat that left the Union commander, General Henry Halleck, figuratively and literally holding an empty bag.

Unfortunately for General Beauregard, to President Davis the retreat from Corinth looked suspiciously like the retreats being performed by Joe Johnston in Virginia. To make matters worse, Beauregard never took the time to sufficiently explain his reasons for the withdrawal. Instead, Davis was forced to send one of

General Pierre Gustave Toutant Beauregard, the hero of Fort Sumter. (Library of Congress)

his advisors to Beauregard's headquarters to get information about the army. Before Davis could determine what to do next, Beauregard decided that he needed a couple of weeks of rest and relaxation after the hectic pace of the last few months. Displaying his usual lack of regard for the president, Beauregard delayed until the last minute before sending a letter to Davis informing of his sabbatical. However, as soon as Beauregard left, his second-in-command, General Braxton Bragg, sent a telegram to Davis explaining the situation. Davis's response was equally swift. Beauregard was to be considered absent without leave and Bragg was to take over his responsibilities as commander of the army.

As was the case in his appointment of Lee in Virginia, Davis had very few options available to him. Bragg was readily available and, as Beauregard's second-in-command, already familiar with the condition of the army. Beauregard was extremely upset by his demotion and his future dealings with Davis remained strained for the rest of the war. Beauregard revealed his feelings toward Davis in a letter to a friend stating, "If the country be satisfied to have me laid on the shelf by a man who is either demented or a traitor to his high trust—well, let it be so."

Although Bragg would enjoy better relations with President Davis, he had his share of quirks. One undoubtedly apocryphal story that made the rounds was that Bragg, then a lieutenant commanding several companies, submitted a requisition for supplies, which he subsequently denied in his capacity as quartermaster. Bragg then submitted the entire matter to the post commander who remarked, "My God Mr. Bragg, you have quarreled with every officer in the army, and now you are quarreling with yourself!" It was also rumored that his men had tried to kill him during the Mexican War by tossing an exploding 12-pound shell under his cot. Bragg survived without a scratch, but the tent was demolished. Once Bragg had become one of the full generals of the Confederacy, however, his quirks were no longer just grist for soldierly gossip—they became a problem for President Jefferson Davis.

The Third Crisis in Command:
Utter Defeat for Braxton Bragg

Shortly after being given command of the Confederate Army of Mississippi, Bragg's command was enlarged and his army renamed the Army of Tennessee. Bragg responded to this vote of confidence from President Davis by planning and carrying out an 800-mile march from his base in Mississippi to Chattanooga, Tennessee, and preparing for an invasion of Kentucky. The invasion went well at first, but then a combination of a lack of water, a lack of cooperation with his subordinate commanders, and an unexpected lack of nerve from Bragg himself, doomed the expedition. After a bloody but inconsequential battle at Perryville, Kentucky, Bragg decided to withdraw back to Middle Tennessee. Although Bragg declared the campaign a success, his inability to achieve any long-term gains marked the campaign, in the minds of most, as a terrible failure. Bragg's next offensive effort also ended in a bloody, drawn battle at Murfreesboro, Tennessee. He was then defeated, this time bloodlessly, in the Tullahoma Campaign when he was completely outmaneuvered by the Union army commanded by General William Rosecrans. Not only did Bragg have to withdraw from Chattanooga, he was forced to pull out of Tennessee completely. For most Civil War generals, three straight defeats would have either ended or severely derailed a career. Yet President Davis, for a lack of better options, stuck with Braxton Bragg and even sent him reinforcements in the fall of 1863, with hopes of winning an elusive victory in the West.

General Braxton Bragg commanded the Confederate Army of Tennessee for much of the war. (Library of Congress)

For once, Bragg repaid Davis with a smashing victory. Using the reinforcements sent from General Lee's army in Virginia, Bragg nearly destroyed the Union Army of the Cumberland at the battle of Chickamauga. Only a stubborn rearguard action at Snodgrass Hill, conducted by General George Thomas, allowed the bulk of Rosecrans's beaten army to withdraw successfully to Chattanooga. However, Bragg did not have much time to savor his victory. Angered by Bragg's unwillingness to aggressively follow up his victory, General Nathan Bedford Forrest confronted him shortly afterwards: "You have played the part of a…scoundrel, and are a coward, and if you were any part of a man I would slap your jowls and force you to resent it." Bragg was also having difficulty with his second-in-command, General Leonidas Polk. Realizing that the former bishop was not up to the job of corps command, Bragg tried to get rid of Polk almost as soon as he was given command of the army. However, his efforts were blocked by the seniority-conscious President Davis, who refused "citing various legal technicalities" that could not be overlooked. When Bragg finally took matters in his own hands and sent Polk packing for his execrable performance at Chickamauga, Davis knew he had to act.

Realizing that the only two alternatives available to him should he decide to remove Bragg from command were Beauregard or Johnston, President Davis devised a plan that he was sure would shore up Bragg's support in the Army of Tennessee. Davis himself traveled to meet with Bragg and his officers at their headquarters overlooking Chattanooga. After convening an extraordinary council of war, Davis asked each of the generals present whether they still had faith in Bragg's ability to command, confident that none would be so bold as to denounce their commanding officer in such a public manner. Davis was wrong. With Bragg sitting silently in the corner, each of his top generals called for his removal in the strongest of terms. Even though his plan had gone dangerously off course, Davis was still unwilling to reinstate Beauregard or Johnston to command the army. With his hands tied by his own adherence to military protocol, Davis left Bragg in command. The results were disastrous—complete and utter defeat in the battle of Chattanooga. Not only did Bragg's men not defend their seemingly impregnable defensive positions, many simply ran away and didn't stop until they were safely in Georgia. It was a defeat that was unprecedented in the Confederate army, and Davis could not ignore it. Bragg was sacked, and Joe Johnston was reinstated as the commander of the Army of Tennessee.

The Fourth Crisis in Command:
Joe Johnston Retreats Again

President Davis's reticence to return Joe Johnston to command proved well-founded during the summer campaign of 1864. At a time when the Confederacy desperately needed military victories, especially in the face of upcoming Northern elections, Johnston seemed stuck in reverse. Twice he seemed prepared to strike out at General Sherman's advancing army—the first time when it crossed the Oostanaula River and the second when the Etowah River was crossed—but both times the attacks failed to materialize. When Johnston gave up his strong position astride the Chattahoochee River on July 5, 1864, Davis began considering the possibility of replacing Johnston yet again. The problem, as usual, was who to replace him with. Davis toyed with the idea of sending Lee out west, but he had his hands full with General Grant in Virginia. The other usual suspects were Bragg, who had been disgraced after Chattanooga, or Beauregard, who Davis considered little better than Johnston. For the second time in the war, Davis considered candidates who were not among the five full generals appointed in 1861.

General William Hardee was the most senior general available to replace Johnston, and Davis's natural instinct was to respect seniority if at all possible. However, Braxton Bragg had other ideas. Since his removal from active command, Bragg had served as Davis's top military advisor, and when Davis became convinced that Johnston was going to give up Atlanta without a fight, he sent Bragg to investigate the situation. Bragg's conclusion was that General John Bell Hood was the right man for the job. After hesitating briefly, Davis gave the order. John Bell Hood was now the new commander of the Army of Tennessee. To get around the seniority issue, Davis gave Hood a temporary promotion to full general.

President Davis's decision to go outside the strict bounds of seniority came back to haunt him almost immediately. Unlike Joe Johnston, Hood was unafraid to attack Sherman's army. Three times within the first 11 days of taking command Hood hurled his army at the enemy, and three times he failed. Finally, Davis had to order Hood to retire to the defenses of Atlanta and to try to hold the city for as long as possible without getting trapped. Even after losing more than 20,000 men

A Currier and Ives print showing General Joe Johnston surrendering the last major Confederate army, in North Carolina, to General W.T. Sherman. (Library of Congress)

in three failed attacks, Hood was not inclined to remain on the defensive and attacked Sherman's army yet again, when his only remaining railroad lifeline to Atlanta (about 20 miles away, in Jonesborough) was threatened. Once more Hood's attack ended in failure, and he was forced to withdraw his men from Atlanta. Even after this fourth defeat, Hood was still not ready to give up the offensive. After conferring with Davis, Hood received permission to lead his men on an impracticable quest into Tennessee, with the goal of recapturing Nashville—perhaps the most heavily guarded city outside of Washington. Yet again, Hood led his men to disaster. First at the battle of Franklin, where Hood lined them up for a charge that was larger and grander than Pickett's Charge at Gettysburg—and equally fruitless. By the time Hood finally reached Nashville, it was December. Against all logic, Hood deployed his underfed and ill-clad men around the city and waited for the inevitable Union attack. When the attack came, Hood's once proud army was shattered.

After gathering the remnants of his army and guiding them back to Georgia, Hood quietly resigned his command. His days as a soldier were over. Not surprisingly, President Davis once again appointed Joe Johnston to take command of what was left of the Army of Tennessee, and Johnston remained in that position until the war ended. Although Johnston's tenure as commander in the West can be considered the least debilitating of the group, it can in no way be considered successful. The fact that Davis repeatedly appointed him to command, despite his well-known deficiencies, speaks volumes for the failure of the Confederate military to identify, nurture, and promote young talent. When the war ended, the Confederacy had stuck with the same group of generals for the entire war: Samuel Cooper, Robert E. Lee, Joe Johnston, and Pierre Gustave Toutant Beauregard—the men President Davis appointed in 1861. However, the top generals in the Union army were Ulysses S. Grant, William Tecumseh Sherman, and Phil Sheridan—all little-known and little-regarded in 1861. The primary reason for this was President Lincoln's willingness to remove generals from command who were unsuccessful. Generals such as Irvin McDowell, George McClellan, John Pope, and Joseph Hooker were either sitting at home when the war ended or serving in some backwater command far from the front lines. In the end, President Davis's almost slavish devotion to the concept of seniority created the same stagnancy at the top level of the command structure that had plagued the prewar Federal army. Lacking the ability to rise to the rank necessary to command an army, scores of qualified and efficient corps, division, and brigade commanders were never able to make their mark in the war the way Grant, Sherman, and Sheridan did for the Union army. Most would probably have failed, but by continuing to turn to men like Joe Johnston and Braxton Bragg, the Confederacy was never able to find its diamond in the rough who might have led them to victory.

THE CIVIL WAR HALL OF SHAME: COMMANDERS WITH BAD TIMING, BAD JUDGEMENT, AND BAD LUCK

Edward Baker: Blind Man's Bluff

Always an adventure-seeker, Edward Dickenson Baker led an Illinois regiment during the Black War in 1832 and commanded a brigade during the Mexican War, 14 years later. Drawn westward by the gold rush, Baker ended up moving to Oregon. After organizing the state's Republican party, Baker was elected the new state's first senator. However, Baker's biggest claim to fame was the friendship he had struck up with Abraham Lincoln while both had been lawyers in Illinois. They became such good friends that Lincoln named his second son Edward Baker Lincoln. Senator Baker also rode in Lincoln's carriage on inauguration day and introduced him to the audience for his first speech as president.

When the war started, Lincoln offered Baker an appointment as major general. However, the politically astute Baker turned him down, preferring to raise a regiment of his own in Pennsylvania and accept a commission as its colonel. The reason for Baker's refusal was that if he became a general, he would have to resign his Senate seat. As a colonel, Baker could and did ride directly from the field to his seat in the Senate chamber, stopping only to unbuckle his sword and pistol belt. Baker's regiment served in a brigade commanded by General Charles Stone. On October 21, 1861, Stone was ordered to send a force across the Potomac River to determine if Confederate forces were still occupying the town of Leesburg, Virginia. Baker's river crossing at Ball's Bluff proceeded very slowly, because only three small boats were available to ferry the men and, once they were across the Potomac River, there was only a small cow path to the top of the steep bluff.

Despite only having orders to "make a slight demonstration," Baker pushed his entire regiment across the river. Once across, Baker was delighted to discover that his men had run into some Confederate defenders. But Baker's delight turned to dismay when a Confederate volley disabled one of his cannons and the other rolled back down the bluff and into the river, after firing only one shot. Lacking artillery, Baker tried to rally his troops and was almost immediately shot in the head and killed. After Baker's death, his men panicked and tried to make it back to the boats. In their urgency to get across the river, all three boats were swamped, and the survivors were shot as they tried to swim to safety. In all, more than 200 Union soldiers were killed or wounded, and another 700 were missing and presumed drowned. Among those captured were the grandson of Paul Revere, the son of Oliver Wendell Holmes, and the nephew of James Russell Lowell.

Such a terrible travesty, coming hard on the heals of the disaster at Bull Run, couldn't be ignored. Because Senator Baker had been killed, General Stone found himself the chief target of a new investigative board set up by Congress. When the Joint Committee on the Conduct of the War was finished, they were convinced that Stone had deliberately ordered his men into an ambush, and he was arrested and imprisoned. Stone, who had been a West Point graduate and teacher, was eventually released for lack of evidence six months later without ever being formally charged of a crime. He sat in Washington for months waiting for orders, despite requests for his services from Generals Banks, Hooker, and Grant. Stone resigned in disgust in 1864 and went to Egypt to became chief of the Khedive's (the ruler of Egypt) general staff. He was later made Pasha (provincial governor) until his retirement in 1883.

A drawing, by F.O.C. Darley, of the death of Colonel Edward Baker at Ball's Bluff, Virginia. (Library of Congress)

Jefferson C. Davis: Getting Away With Murder

Jefferson Columbus Davis (who was no relation to the Confederate president) joined the Union army as a private during the Mexican War, where he earned a rare battlefield commission as lieu-tenant. He found himself in Fort Sumter at the beginning of the Civil War, and was promoted to captain for bravery under fire. Davis was quickly promoted again and served as a colonel and brigade commander at Wilson's Creek and a division commander at Pea Ridge. In May 1862, Davis was promoted to brigadier general and ordered to help General "Bull" Nelson organize the defenses at Louisville, Kentucky. It was evident from the start that Nelson, a huge ex-navy midshipman, and the diminutive Davis would not get along. Eventually, Nelson ordered Davis to leave the department. Davis did leave, but returned several days later to demand satisfaction. He approached Nelson at the Galt Hotel,

Union General Jefferson C. Davis rose from the ranks to become a brigadier general in the Union army. (Library of Congress)

but was dismissed and called an "insolent puppy." Davis responded by throwing a piece of paper in Nelson's face, whereupon Nelson backhanded Davis across the room. Nelson then went up the stairs of the hotel towards his room. He was at his door when Davis called out his name. When Nelson turned around, Davis shot him in the chest. Within a half hour, Bull Nelson was dead.

In addition to being a friend of President Lincoln, Nelson had been one of the Union heroes of Shiloh. After his death, General Buell had Davis arrested, but did not have enough spare officers to convene a court-martial. He requested that a commission be appointed to investigate the shooting, but no charges were ever filed. A grand jury in Louisville did indict Davis for manslaughter, but he was released on bail and reported back to his unit. Jefferson Davis had gotten away with murder, but his saga was not complete. On December 7, 1864, Davis was commanding a corps during Sherman's march to the sea, when he came to Ebenezer Creek. Because the creek was too deep and wide to ford, Davis had his engineers construct a pontoon bridge. As was the case throughout the march, Sherman's columns were followed by thousands of freed slaves. These camp followers irritated Davis, and he ordered the bridge pulled up after his men had crossed. When the freed slaves realized they were being left behind, many attempted to swim across the creek. While a few made it to the other side, most drowned in the attempt.

The situation was made worse when Confederate cavalry swooped down on the crowd gathered at the water's edge and forced dozens more into the creek. Before it was over, scores were drowned and the rest were rounded up and forced back into servitude. For his part, Sherman never disciplined Davis for his actions and he continued to serve as a corps commander for the duration of the war. Davis did suffer slightly for his actions in that he was never promoted past the rank of brigadier general, his rank at the time of Nelson's murder.

Nathan Shanks Evans: Drunk and Disorderly

Nathan Evans, an 1848 graduate of West Point, had won renown as a skilled Indian fighter in the 1850s, before resigning his commission when his home state of South Carolina seceded. After obtaining a commission as a colonel in the Confederate army, the 37-year-old found himself on the extreme end of the Confederate line at the battle of Manassas. From his position, Evans was able to detect the Union's turning movement and threw men across the stone bridge over Bull Run. His brigade, along with several others, held off the Union attack until reinforcements arrived on the field. Evans was hailed as one of the heroes of Manassas, but did not garner a promotion, due to his reputation as a heavy drinker. One witness said that Evans had assigned an aide to carry a small keg of whiskey for his use during the battle. Shortly after Manassas, Evans earned the thanks of the Confederate Congress for his role in the spectacular victory at Ball's Bluff. However, that victory was also tainted, because Evans had never actually taken the field during the battle, and one of his officers, Colonel Eppa Hunton, complained that Evans had been "drinking freely during the day."

Union soldiers retreat into the Potomac River after being defeated by Colonel Nathan Evans's forces at Ball's Bluff, from The Illustrated London News. *(Library of Congress)*

Despite the rumors, Evans was promoted to brigadier general and given command of a brigade of South Carolina troops. However, his harsh and erratic behavior continued to hamper his military career. After the battle of Second Manassas, Evans became embroiled in a dispute with General John Bell Hood over the possession of several captured ambulances. When the campaign was over, Evans was transferred to South Carolina. He performed well at the battle of Secessionville but was unable to get along with his superiors, and his brigade was again transferred. In North Carolina, Evans's brigade ran into an advancing Federal column near Kinston. Severely outnumbered, Evans's men put up a stiff fight until Union artillery fire forced his left flank to retreat. Evans, who was probably drunk, got confused in the retreat and forgot about the rest of his troops when he ordered the bridge he was protecting over the Neuse River to be burned. To make matters worse, he mistakenly ordered artillery fire against the troops he left stranded and they were forced to surrender.

Dogged by rumors that he had been intoxicated during the battle, Evans and his brigade—now dubbed the "Tramp Brigade," were transferred to Tennessee, and Evans was court-martialed for disobeying orders and excessive drinking. He was acquitted of the charges, but his military career was in a tailspin. Transferred again to South Carolina, Evans was relieved of duty by General Beauregard, who considered him incompetent. Shortly after that, he was injured in a fall from his horse and saw no further combat. After the war, Evans became a teacher and headmaster at a school in Midway, Alabama, for three years before his death in 1868, at the age of 44.

James Ledlie: Bombed at the Crater

James Hewitt Ledlie was a 29-year-old civil engineer from Utica, New York, with no military experience when the Civil War began. Through his political connections, Ledlie got himself appointed as a major and then promoted to lieutenant colonel of the Third New York Artillery Regiment in 1862. In December 1862, Ledlie saw his first combat outside Kinston, North Carolina. The first shot from his battery "carried away half the head of a man in Company D," and killed him instantly. Ledlie fared even worse the next day when he ordered his cannoneers to cut the fuses of their shells too short. As a result, the shells exploded over the heads of friendly troops instead of over the Confederate lines. For his efforts, Ledlie was promoted to brigadier general.

In May 1864, Ledlie was transferred to command of a brigade in the Ninth Corps of the Army of the Potomac. In his first action as an infantry commander, a drunken Ledlie led his men across the North Anna River at Ox Ford and ordered an assault against an entrenched Confederate position. Ledlie's men were stopped in their tracks by a Confederate volley, routed, and forced back. Ledlie's own aide-de-camp was among those captured, along with the regimental colors. Instead of being reprimanded for this lapse of judgment, Ledlie was promoted to divisional command by General Ambrose Burnside. Ledlie managed to avoid making any more gaffes until July 1864, when Burnside appointed him to lead another assault. The plan was for Union engineers to build a tunnel under the Confederate lines outside Petersburg, Virginia; fill the tunnel with black power; and blow open a hole wide enough for Union troops to capture the city. Burnside originally tapped General Edward Ferrero, who commanded a division of African-American troops, to lead the attack but was ordered to make a change by General Grant, who thought the operation too risky for the un-

Union General James Ledlie loved the bottle more than he did leading troops into battle. (Library of Congress)

tried black infantrymen. Burnside had his remaining generals draw straws to determine who would lead the charge. Ledlie drew the short straw.

The mine exploded at 4:45 a.m., creating a crater 170 feet long, 80 feet wide, and 30 feet deep. Nine Confederate companies were blown into the air, and more than 200 rebel soldiers were instantly killed. Ledlie's men rushed forward toward the gap in the lines but, instead of going around the huge crater, they marched straight into it. When the line officers realized what was happening they looked to their commanding officer for orders. However, Ledlie wasn't there. Instead of leading his men, Ledlie was several hundred yards behind the lines, drinking medicinal rum with General Ferrero in a bombproof shelter. Additional Union reinforcements poured into the crater until, by 8:30 a.m., more than 15,000 were trapped in its unfriendly confines. The Confederate counterattack turned into a turkey shoot, and more than 4,000 Union men were killed or wounded before the crater could be evacuated, in what General Grant called "a stupendous failure." In the aftermath, the military careers of Burnside, Ledlie, and Ferrero came to an end. Ledlie escaped being court-martialed, but only because he agreed to resign his commission. According to his obituary, Ledlie was offered a commission in the regular army after the war, but declined, in order to continue his engineering career. As successful in civilian affairs as he was a failure in the military, Ledlie specialized in the construction of railroad bridges and trestles for the Union Pacific Railroad in the postwar period. At the time of his death he had risen to the position of chief engineer of the California and Nevada Railroad and president of the Baltimore, Cincinnati, and Western Railroad Construction Company.

John Newton: Engineering Defeat in Florida

John Newton graduated second in the West Point class of 1842 and began his military career in the Engineering Corps constructing fortifications and lighthouses. When the Civil War began, the Virginia-born Newton decided to remain loyal to the Union, much to the dismay of his friends and family, and was rewarded with a commission as a brigadier general. Newton's military career began to derail shortly after the battle of Fredericksburg when he joined with a group of generals who had serious doubts about General Burnside's military skills. Newton, accompanied by former congressman General Cochrane, left camp shortly after the battle, determined to bring their complaints directly to Washington. When Burnside learned of the visit, he issued orders dismissing Newton, along with his fellow conspirators, Generals Franklin, Brooks, and Cochrane for "going directly to the President of the United States with criticisms upon the plans of their commanding officer." In addition, he ordered the immediate transfer of five other generals he suspected of being sympathetic to the conspirators. Rather than disrupting the entire officer corps of the Army of the Potomac, Lincoln chose to replace Burnside.

At first it looked like most of the generals involved in the incident would get away with their actions, as only General William Franklin was relieved of command for being part of the anti-Burnside cabal. However, within a few months, General Brooks's promotion to major general was revoked, and he was forced to retire. General Cochrane, fearing he too would be targeted, resigned his commission and returned to politics. Newton also saw his promotion to major general revoked, despite his good service at Gettysburg, where he commanded the First Corps after General Reynolds was killed. Newton was then transferred to General Sherman's army in Georgia. After participating in the Atlanta campaign, Newton was again transferred despite performing well. This time he was sent to the Department of Key West and the Dry Tortugas. In 15 months, Newton had gone from commanding a corps in the Army of the Potomac to overseeing an island prison and a sandy stretch of beach.

Unwilling to sit idly by while the Civil War drew to a close, Newton hatched a plan that he hoped would lead to the capture of

Union General John Newton led the Army of the Potomac's I Corps at Gettysburg. (Library of Congress)

the Florida state capital in Tallahassee. Newton obtained permission to land a small force at St. Marks, 20 miles south of Tallahassee, but bad weather delayed the expedition long enough for local militia in the area to gather. When Newton learned that all the planks had been pulled up from the bridge over the St. Marks River at Newport, he marched his men north to a spot where a natural bridge over the river was located. However, when Newton reached the natural bridge, he discovered Confederate forces had beaten him there as well. When attempts to find another river crossing failed, Newton ordered a full scale assault.

The strong Confederate defensive position, backed by superior artillery, turned Newton's attack into a dreadful failure. In addition, the Confederate line was bolstered by a group of cadets from the Florida Military Institute and a detachment from the West Florida Seminary (now Florida State University). After two more unsuccessful charges, Newton finally gave up. In the day's fighting, the small Union force lost more than a hundred men, and their casualty rate was one of the highest of the war. With his last hope of redeeming his military career gone, Newton resorted to the tactic that had brought him to Florida in the first place. He blamed someone else. According to Newton's official report, the defeat was not caused by his rash and unsupported attack, but by the navy which "didn't cooperate" and failed to "land a force of seaman" on the other side of the St. Marks River.

Thomas Selfridge: Best Swimmer in the Navy

Thomas Selfridge was born into a naval family. Following in the footsteps of his father, who had joined the navy in 1818, Selfridge graduated first in his class from the United States Naval Academy in Annapolis, in 1854. He was promoted to lieutenant in 1860 and was serving aboard the USS *Cumberland*, a fighting sloop and one of the last sail-powered vessels in the U.S. Navy, when the Civil War began. Selfridge commanded one of the forward 10-inch pivot guns during the victorious bombardment of Forts Clark and Hatteras, on the North Carolina coast in 1861. However, Selfridge and the USS *Cumberland* did not fare so well in 1862 when they came face to face with the CSS *Virginia*, the first Confederate ironclad, in Hampton Roads. Although Selfridge and his shipmates raked the CSS *Virginia* with cannon fire, the shells just bounced off her 4-inch iron plating. With the ship going down, Selfridge managed to escape by jumping out of a gunport and swimming to a nearby launch, but a third of the USS *Cumberland's* 120-man crew was not so lucky and went down with the ship.

Selfridge got his first independent command shortly after the sinking of the USS *Cumberland*. However, instead of being given one of the navy's new ironclad gunboats, Selfridge was made captain of an experimental "submarine propeller" boat. It was the hope of Assistant Naval Secretary Gustavus Fox that Selfridge could take the USS *Alligator* up the James River and destroy a Confederate ironclad that was nearing completion in Richmond. If he was successful, Fox promised to make Selfridge a captain. Selfridge had the USS *Alligator* towed into New York Harbor and was able to remain submerged and to resurface without difficulties. However, when he took the USS *Alligator* for her first cruise, he discovered that the propulsion system was defective. In addition, the submarine suddenly started to sink. Selfridge got the crew on deck and they drifted helplessly down the river until a passing schooner towed them to safety.

Shortly after his unsuccessful stint commanding the submarine propeller boat, Selfridge was promoted to lieutenant commander and given command of the USS *Cairo,* an ironclad gunboat. A very strict commander, his first rule was forbidding any and all "profane swearing." In December 1862, the USS *Cairo* was ordered to accompany a fleet of rams (ships specially designed to ram into enemy ships) up the Yazoo River near Vicksburg, Mississippi. When the rams, commanded by Colonel Charles Ellet, suddenly stopped, Selfridge ordered them forward even though Ellet had warned him that enemy torpedoes (underwater mines) had been spotted in the river. Selfridge then ordered the USS *Cairo* to take the lead and continued to advance up the river until two explosions stopped him for good. Within 12 minutes the USS *Cairo* sank, becoming the first ship ever to be sunk by an electrically detonated torpedo. Fortunately, the river was very shallow and no hands were lost, but the aggressive Selfridge was admonished by his commanding officer for "disobeying orders."

Selfridge expected to be court-martialed for losing the USS *Cairo*, but the navy didn't have enough trained officers, and he was instead given command of the USS *Conestoga*. His new vessel was originally a civilian side-wheel steamboat but had been acquired by the military and converted into a 570-ton timberclad river gunboat. Confined to routine river patrol service, Selfridge and the USS *Conestoga* seemed relatively safe—until March 1864, when she collided with the USS *General Price* and sank in the Ouachita River. Miraculously, the USS *General Price*, which was carrying a load of ammunition, didn't detonate and once again Selfridge managed to swim to safety.

Despite having lost his last two ships, Selfridge continued to serve in the navy. He performed well during the Red River campaign and was given command of the USS *Huron* in 1865, which took part in the bombardment on Fort Fisher, located on the coast of North Carolina. He continued in the service after the war and was promoted to the rank of commander. He retired in 1898, with a rank of rear admiral and a perfect record; in his 47-year naval career, Selfridge never managed to sink a single enemy vessel.

Earl Van Dorn: Victim of Love

A cousin of President Andrew Jackson, Earl Van Dorn graduated from West Point in 1842, served as a cavalryman for 18 years, was wounded four times, and was promoted to major and third ranking officer in the Second U.S. Cavalry, before he resigned his commission when his home state of Mississippi seceded. In June

1861, Van Dorn was appointed as a major general in the Confederate army and, seven months later, was given command of the Department of the Trans-Mississippi. As soon as Van Dorn reached his new command, he began making plans for an offensive that he hoped would take him to St. Louis. However, Van Dorn's army was defeated at the battle of Pea Ridge, in northwest Arkansas, when his supply train was lost and his men ran out of ammunition.

Before Van Dorn had a chance to redeem himself in Arkansas, he was ordered to bring his men to Corinth, Mississippi. Arriving too late to participate in the battle of Shiloh, Van Dorn was then given command of the defenses at Vicksburg. Not content to remain on the defensive, the ever-aggressive Van Dorn organized an attack on Baton Rouge, Louisiana. This attack also failed and resulted in the loss of the CSS *Arkansas*—the only Confederate ironclad operating on the Mississippi River. Van Dorn's final opportunity to command an army ended in disaster in October 1862, when he launched a frontal attack against the Union fortifications at Corinth, Mississippi. After the battle, Van Dorn was relieved of command and summoned before a court of inquiry to answer charges that he had been drunk on duty, that he had neglected the wounded, and that he had failed to provide himself with an accurate map.

Van Dorn was acquitted of all charges by a friendly court that concluded the charges had not been sufficiently proven. Remembering Van Dorn's reputation as a fine horseman, President Jefferson Davis reassigned him to command the cavalry forces at Vicksburg. Once there, he again immediately went on the offensive, but this time the results were a smashing success. Van Dorn not only succeeded in destroying the Union supply base at Holly Springs, Mississippi, he stopped General Grant's Vicksburg campaign in its tracks and caused the failure of General Sherman's (now unsupported) expedition down the Mississippi River, as well. Two years into the war, Van Dorn had found his niche as a cavalry commander. After his success at Holly Springs, he was promoted to command of the entire cavalry corps operating in Middle Tennessee. Van Dorn scored another victory at Thompson's Station on March 5, 1863, which cemented his reputation as a skilled cavalry commander.

Not all of General Van Dorn's conquests occurred on the battlefield. An avowed ladies' man, Van Dorn was as skilled with a paintbrush as he was with a sword. He was also an amateur poet and "a dedicated romantic." His reputation led one young widow to warn him to "let the ladies alone until the war was over." To which Van Dorn responded, "I cannot do that, for that is what I am fighting for." Van Dorn met his match when he met and fell for a 25-year-old married women named Jessie Helen McKissack Peters. Described as incredibly beautiful, Jessie Peters was the third wife of a 49-year-old doctor who had been away from home for nearly a year while serving in the state legislature. Rumors of a romantic relationship between his wife and Van Dorn, including late night visits and long unchaperoned carriage rides, greeted Dr. Peters when he returned to Spring Hill in April 1863. Taking matters into his own hands, Dr. Peters went to Van Dorn's headquarters and shot him from behind, while the general was working at his desk. The grievously wounded cavalry officer survived for a little more than four hours before he died without regaining consciousness.

Confederate General Earl Van Dorn led his army to defeat at the Battle of Corinth, Mississippi. Print by Kurz & Allison. (Library of Congress)

Felix Zollicoffer: Nearsighted Newspaperman

Felix Zollicoffer had already risen from journeyman printer to associate editor of the *Nashville Republican Banner* when he decided to enter the world of politics. After serving as comptroller and state senator in Tennessee, Zollicoffer served four terms in the House of Representatives before resigning to join the Confederate army. Although Zollicoffer's only military experience had been as a lieutenant in the Second Seminole War, Governor Isham Harris gave him a commission as a brigadier general and command of the Confederate forces in eastern Tennessee. In January 1862, Zollicoffer was ordered to move his small army to Mill Springs and set up his camp on the south side of the Cumberland River. However, Zollicoffer could not find enough flat ground for his 4,000-man campsite and decided to set up his camp on the opposite side of the river.

When General George Crittenden learned that Zollicoffer had selected a location with a wide river at his back and from which he could not easily retreat, Crittenden rushed to the scene. To make matters worse, a large Union force commanded by Union General George Thomas was camped only 9 miles away. Fearing disaster should Thomas attack, Crittenden decided to attack Thomas first. The disorganized attack was bogged down in a driving rain that rendered most of the Confederate's old flintlocks inoperable. Zollicoffer, wearing a bright white raincoat, attempted to rally his men, but got disoriented and rode straight toward the Union lines. The nearsighted general, who had forgotten to wear his glasses, began shouting orders at a Union officer who, realizing that Zollicoffer was a Confederate, shot him in the chest. When Zollicoffer fell, the defeat turned into a rout as the Confederate soldiers rushed back to the Cumberland River. Using an old stern-wheeler, the soldiers managed to get across the river, but left behind all their artillery and wagons.

Despite the fact that the Confederate disaster at Mill Springs was caused almost entirely by the faulty troop disposition of the inexperienced Zollicoffer, blame for the defeat fell squarely on General Crittenden's shoulders. Crittenden, whose brother was a Union officer, was sent before a court of inquiry and charged with treason and being "in an almost beastly state of intoxication" during the battle. Although Crittenden was found innocent of the most serious charge of treason, he was found guilty of being intoxicated and reduced to the rank of colonel. Crittenden eventually resigned from the Confederate army and spent the rest of the war as a civilian staff officer. For his part, Zollicoffer was hailed as a fallen hero. Or, as one popular song put it: "A name in song and story, he died on the field of glory."

The Death of Zollicoffer. Oil painting by D. Johnson. (Author's Collection)

PART THREE

THE FIGHTING

After Atlanta fell, inflation in the Confederacy, which had been dropping through most of 1864, skyrocketed to astronomical proportions. This was conclusive evidence that the loss of Atlanta and the ensuing reelection of President Lincoln ended any lingering hopes of victory that the Southern people may have had. It is also one of the reasons the battle of Atlanta was one of the most influential battles of the Civil War. Another influential battle took place at Glorieta Pass, New Mexico and ended any hopes of expanding the Confederacy beyond it's prewar boundaries. Rather than focusing on the massive, bloody, and relatively fruitless battles that took place in Virginia, this section of the book analyzes battles and campaigns with enduring consequences. These battles and campaigns—the most influential of the war—fostered irrevocable changes, which strongly impacted the conduct and outcome of the war.

CHAPTER 7

THE MOST INFLUENTIAL BATTLES OF THE CIVIL WAR

Manassas: The First Major Victory of the War

When the war began, most people believed that it would be a short affair. In the South, men and boys energized by the great victory at Fort Sumter rushed to join up, so as not to miss out on any of the fun, firm in their belief that the Yankees "would run like sheep" at the first sign of battle. In the North, patriotic crowds heartily responded to newspaper headlines declaring "On to Richmond." When the Union military commander General Winfield Scott proposed a patient strategy that involved blockading the South and slowly suffocating the Confederacy, it was dismissed out of hand and derisively referred to as the Anaconda Plan. At the behest of President Lincoln and against his own better judgment, Scott organized a 35,000-man army, comprised mainly of raw recruits and commanded by a man (General Irvin McDowell) with no prior experience in the field, and sent them south to attack the Confederate army guarding the railhead at Manassas, Virginia.

Fearing his men were too weary from their march when they approached Manassas on August 18, 1861, McDowell decided to postpone the attack for three days. The delay was crucial, because it allowed General Joe Johnston to transfer 10,000 men from his army in nearby Winchester to Manassas in time to join the battle. The Confederates were also aided by McDowell's unwieldy battle plan, which included a long daylight march on the day of the battle and gave the Confederates ample time to prepare.

Despite all these hardships, McDowell's men fought hard and came very close to carrying the day. However, the stubborn defense put up by the men of General Thomas J. Jackson (soon to be dubbed "Stonewall" Jackson) slowed the Union attack, and a sudden counterattack by General J.E.B. Stuart's cavalry regiment forced the Union army to withdraw. The withdrawal quickly turned into a rout, giving the Confederates a stunning victory, which paid dividends to the Confederacy that resonated long after echoes of the final volley died away.

The immediate fallout was swift and decisive. President Lincoln signed two bills calling for an additional million Union recruits, and General George McClellan was called to Washington to command the reconstituted Army of the Potomac. George Templeton Strong, a prominent New Yorker, proclaimed that the anniversary of the battle would forever be remembered as Black Monday, and Horace Greeley, the editor of the *New York Tribune* and one of the most vocal proponents of an early attack, wrote a letter urging President Lincoln not to shrink from making peace with the rebels "on their own terms."

The weeping and wailing in the North was answered by even louder shouts of jubilation in the South. Thomas Cobb, a member of the newly formed Confederate Congress, called Manassas "one of the decisive battles of the world." Ardent secessionist Edmund Ruffin believed that the hard-fought victory would be "virtually the close of the war." Although Ruffin was incorrect in this assessment, the victory at Manassas did have an enormous impact on how the war would play out, at least in the East. According to historian James McPherson, "The confidence gained by the men who won at Manassas imbued them with an esprit de corps.... At the same time the Union defeat instilled a gnawing, half acknowledged sense of martial inferiority among northern officers in the Virginia theater." Victory in the first major battle of the war reinforced the belief held by many Confederate soldiers that they were invincible while, at the same time, defeat established a strong element of doubt and despair, in the minds of Union soldiers, that wouldn't be wiped away until the great Union victory at Gettysburg almost two years later.

Ruins of the Henry House after the Confederate victory at the battle of Manassas. (Library of Congress)

Throughout the history of warfare, the outcome of the first battle is of paramount importance because it provides the winning side with what one historian calls a "force multiplier" that is extremely difficult to dislodge. Hannibal used this phenomenon to great advantage during the Second Punic War, when he parlayed his early victory at the battle of Trevie River, in 217 B.C., into a campaign that brought the Carthaginians to the brink of victory against the powerful Roman Empire. The American army took advantage of this phenomenon during the Mexican War when early victories by the army commanded by General Zachary Taylor, were turned into a swift military campaign that ended in the capture of Mexico City, despite the fact that the Americans were severely outnumbered and the Mexicans firmly entrenched in virtually every subsequent battle. It was also demonstrated in World War II, where early German and Japanese victories led to several years of almost nonstop military conquests.

While the Confederate victory at Manassas gave them an advantage in the East, the opposite occurred in the Western Theater when early victories by the army, commanded by General Grant at Fort Donelson and Shiloh, gave the "force multiplier" advantage to the Union. In fact, during the entire war, the Union army would only lose one major battle in the West (Chickamauga) in which they were not attacking a heavily fortified position. Obviously, winning the first battle is no guarantee of actually winning the war; history is replete with examples, such as the Civil War, when this is not the case. But especially in an era where armies were made up of citizen-soldiers and not highly trained professional soldiers, the psychological advantage gained by early victories cannot be overlooked.

Fort Donelson: Birthplace of Unconditional Surrender Grant

When President Jefferson Davis had to choose a commander for the vast western frontier that stretched from the Great Smokie Mountains to the Indian Territory (Oklahoma), he selected General Albert Sidney Johnston. Facing Johnston were three Union armies totaling 150,000 men. Rather than concentrate his army, Johnston chose to spread it out among the river forts that guarded the Mississippi, Cumberland, and Tennessee Rivers. General Leonidas Polk was given command of the lion's share of men stationed in the forts on the Mississippi River north of Memphis, Tennessee. Smaller garrisons were situated on the Cumberland and Tennessee Rivers, including 5,000 green troops split between Forts Henry and Donelson.

Of all the river forts, Fort Henry was probably the worst designed. In fact, one historian described it as "the most poorly designed of any Civil War bastion." It was built on such low ground that even during an ordinary rise in the Tennessee River the entire fort would be under 2 feet of water. The weakness of Fort Henry was well-known to Union General Ulysses Grant and Flag Officer Andrew Foote. However, their request to launch an attack had little chance of being granted by their cautious departmental commander, General Henry Halleck, until his rival, General Don Carlos Buell, scored a surprise victory at Mill Springs, Kentucky. Jealous of Buell's success, Halleck gave Grant and Foote permission to attack Fort Henry.

The river was so high that Foote's gunboats literally floated into Fort Henry, and victory was so swift and complete that Grant's infantrymen weren't even required.

The only drawback was that the fort's commander, realizing that his position was hopeless, sent the 2,500-man garrison overland to Fort Donelson, 12 miles away. Wasting no time after the victory, Grant immediately marched on Donelson and began a siege of the works. After a failed attempt at fighting their way out of Grant's trap, the three Confederate commanders inside the fort convened a bizarre, late-night council of war. General Floyd turned over command to General Pillow who, in turn, passed command to the third ranking officer in the fort, Simon Bolivar Buckner. Generals Floyd and Pillow then sneaked across the Cumberland River in a small boat and fled.

Left to his own devices, Colonel Buckner immediately began negotiations for surrendering the garrison. Buckner, an old friend of Grant, expected lenient terms and was shocked when Grant demanded "unconditional and immediate surrender." Lacking alternatives, Buckner was forced to comply. The loss of Forts Henry and Donelson opened up the Cumberland and Tennessee Rivers to Union gunboats and within days the Confederates were forced to evacuate Nashville, Tennessee, making it the first Confederate state capital to fall. Within weeks, the Union army controlled all of Kentucky and most of Tennessee. Fort Donelson also marked the first major victory for Ulysses Grant. Using bold maneuvers that would become his trademark, Grant sliced a 100-mile wide gash in the Confederate defensive line. It was only the cautiousness of Henry Halleck that prevented Grant from aggressively following up on his great victory. Instead, Halleck sent Grant's army to Pittsburg Landing (Shiloh) with orders to wait for General Buell to arrive with additional reinforcements. The delay proved critical when a reconstituted Confederate army showed up at Shiloh before Buell did.

Currier and Ives print showing General Ulysses S. Grant's troops storming Fort Donelson, Tennessee. (Library of Congress)

Glorieta Pass: On to San Francisco!

When the Civil War began, President Jefferson Davis had more in mind than just independence for the South. He envisioned a Confederacy that stretched across the continent to the Pacific Coast. To that end, in July 1861 he assigned General Henry Sibley to the command of the Department of New Mexico, with instructions to gain control of the forts along the Rio Grande River, all the way up to Santa Fe. Once this was accomplished, Sibley had Davis's permission to proceed all the way to San Francisco.

Sibley gathered his 3,700-man force at Fort Bliss, Texas (El Paso) and, in early January 1862, began his march up the Rio Grande. After marching across more than 100 miles of barren wilderness, Sibley reached Fort Craig. There a relatively large Union force, commanded by General Edward Canby, marched out to face him at nearby Valverde. In a fierce two-day battle, Canby's forces were severely beaten and were only able to return to the safety of their adobe fort under a flag

General Henry Hopkins Sibley commanded the unsuccessful Confederate expedition into New Mexico and Nevada. (Library of Congress)

of truce. Sibley then pushed on upriver and captured Albuquerque and Santa Fe without a struggle. However, Sibley soon realized that blue-coated soldiers were not the only enemy he faced. Expecting "cheers and volunteers," not to mention provisions, after his long march, Sibley instead found that the locals were "profoundly hostile" toward his Texans.

Sibley's depleted and desperate force remained separated from Las Vegas and the Far West only by Fort Union. However, to get there, Sibley had to pass through the small mountain passes of the Sangre Cristo Mountains. After his advance forces were ambushed at Apache Canyon, Sibley pushed forward to Glorieta Pass, only to find that Union reinforcements had arrived in the form of Pike's Peakers from Denver, Colorado. For five long hours the Union and Confederate forces battled it out in a narrow canyon. According to historian Shelby Foote, "Neither [side] could advance, yet both knew that to fall back would be even more fatal than to stay." The stalemate ended when a small party of Pike's Peakers circled around behind the Confederate lines and burned their 85-wagon supply train. The battle, now known as the "Gettysburg of the West," was over. Without food or water, Sibley knew he could not continue the campaign. Retracing his steps, Sibley's beaten force, after an agonizing march, returned to Texas. When he returned, Sibley sent back his report to President Davis: "Except for its geographical position, the Territory of New Mexico is not worth a quarter of the blood and treasure expended in it's conquest." The dream for a Confederate empire that stretched to the Pacific Ocean was over.

New Orleans: Largest City in the Confederacy Is Lost

Before the war, Mansfield Lovell had been the Deputy Street Commissioner of New York City. When the Civil War broke out, the Maryland-born Lovell resigned his position, joined the Confederate army, and was given the thankless task of commanding the defenses of New Orleans. Lovell's task was made even more difficult when all the regular troops assigned to New Orleans were called away to fight at Shiloh. The few militiamen that were left were distributed amongst the small forts guarding the many water approaches to the city. Lovell was made even more acutely aware of the city's defenselessness when a flotilla of Union gunboats, commanded by Flag Officer David Farragut, crossed the bar at the mouth of the Mississippi River and began bombarding Forts Jackson and St. Phillip, two old star-shaped masonry forts defending the mouth of the river.

General Mansfield Lovell commanded the Confederate troops that defended New Orleans. (Library of Congress)

In a last ditch effort to protect the city, Lovell sent down the half-finished ironclad CSS *Louisiana* and a flotilla of smaller gunboats and fireships to bolster the fort's defenses. Farragut countered by attempting to bomb the two forts into rubble. When that failed, Farragut ordered his gunboats to attempt to pass by the forts. Despite fierce resistance, all but two of the Union ships made it safely past the forts. Knowing that further resistance was futile, Lovell evacuated his small force and left New Orleans completely unprotected.

On April 25, 1862, Farragut took possession of New Orleans. After spending several days attempting to "negotiate" a surrender with the mayor, Farragut took matters into his own hands and ordered his men raise the American flag over the public buildings in the city. Within days, General Benjamin Butler's infantry arrived and cemented Union control over what had been the Confederacy's largest city. The Crescent City was not just the largest in the Confederacy, it was the home of more people than any other four Southern cities combined. According to Edward Pollard, who in 1866 wrote *The Lost Cause*, one of the first histories of the Civil War:

> The fall of New Orleans...sorely punished the vanity of the Confederates; annihilated their power in Louisiana; broke up their routes to Texas and the Gulf; closed their access to the richest grain and cattle country in the South; gave to the enemy a new base of operations; and, more than anything else, staggered the confidence of Europe in the fortunes of the Confederacy.

The Seven Days' Battle: What Might Have Been

The situation for the Confederacy in the spring of 1862 was critical. They had lost all of Tennessee in the great battle of Shiloh and the largest city in the Confederacy had been captured with ease by a Union gunboat squadron. In Virginia, General Lee was facing a 100,000-man army, commanded by General George McClellan, that had advanced up the York River Peninsula to a position where they could see the spires of the churches of Richmond, Virginia. Although Lee was new to command, he quickly set about for a way to defeat his foe. Lee was aided by the fact that McClellan was extremely cautious and convinced that he was greatly outnumbered. As he pleaded and cajoled President Lincoln for additional troops, Lee was given time to formulate a plan. First, he sent cavalry commander General J.E.B. Stuart around the Union army. When Stuart announced to Lee that McClellan's right flank was "in the air," (unprotected), Lee sent word to General Stonewall Jackson, then commanding a small army in the Shenandoah Valley, to join him.

Lee's aggressive plan was to engage the center of McClellan's lines, while Jackson swooped around the unprotected right flank of the Union army. But, as was all too often the case in the Civil War, things went wrong almost from the very start. Despite the fact that Jackson had not yet arrived, General A.P. Hill prematurely launched the first attack. As the day's events unfolded, Lee had to watch from a nearby hill as his army failed to make a dent in the Union line along Beaver Dam Creek. Fortunately for Lee, McClellan ordered a withdrawal soon after dark and gave Lee the opportunity to attack again. As on the previous day, the famed "foot cavalry" of the Shenandoah Valley held the key to the day's success, and once again Stonewall Jackson was late. This trend continued for the rest of the Seven Days' Battle. In fact, Stonewall Jackson was either late or did not show up at all five times before it was all over. Jackson's failures were, in the words of one historian, "complete, disastrous and unredeemable."

During the Shenandoah Valley campaign, and then at Fredericksburg, Second Manassas, Antietam, and Chancellorsville, Jackson was as solid and resourceful a commander as there was. However, the Stonewall Jackson of the Seven Days' Battle, was a different man altogether. There is even a separate entry for Jackson in *The Civil War Dictionary* (David McKay, 1959) that describes this phenomenon: "Jackson of the Chickahominy was a phrase used to distinguish the brilliant Jackson of the Valley from the ineffective Stonewall Jackson who failed five times during the Seven Days' battle."

Anxious to make up for his two lost opportunities, Lee made plans for another attack that was designed to prevent the Union army from escaping to the

General George McClellan, mounted on the boom of the Union ironclad USS Galena *with the Battle of Malvern Hill raging in the background. (Library of Congress)*

safety of the gunboats on the James River. Once again, Jackson failed to get his men into the battle. This time he contented himself with rebuilding a bridge, while the battle raged a mile away at Savage Station. Although he had already missed three opportunities to damage General McClellan's Army of the Potomac, Lee had one last chance and he was determined to make the most of it. However, once again his plans were foiled when Jackson failed to get his men into the battle. This time, Jackson simply went to sleep. After encountering light Union resistance at a bridge crossing White Oak Swamp, Jackson took a nap. After rousing himself long enough to eat a biscuit, Jackson told his staff, who had been waiting impatiently for hours for instructions to advance, "Let us at once [go] to bed...and see if tomorrow we cannot do something."

By the time McClellan's army took up a strong defensive position along the crest of Malvern Hill, the game was up. Lee knew it, but couldn't resist taking one last desperate shot at the retreating Union army. Throughout the day, Confederate units attacked the Union stronghold and were bloodily repelled. However, Jackson's men, at the far end of the line, spent another "non-fighting day—their sixth out of seven." When asked if he was going to join the attack, Jackson replied, "General D. H. Hill has just tried it with his whole division and been repulsed; I guess [we] better not try." There have been many explanations for Jackson's strange behavior during that fateful week. There can be no doubt that Jackson was extremely tired. One artillerist described him as being "worn down to the lowest point of flesh consistent with active service." It is clear that Jackson had paid a price for the arduous four months of marching and fighting of the Shenandoah Valley campaign. However, there were also rumors that Jackson, feeling that his men had been doing all the fighting in Virginia, was content to let the fighting in this campaign fall to someone else. There is also the possibility that Jackson was just not comfortable operating in a subordinate role. Throughout his previous service in the Valley, he had held sole command of his troops. Indeed, twice during the Seven Days' Battle, it appeared that Jackson was content to obey the letter of his instructions and, when they were accomplished, would wait where he was for additional orders. At White Oak Swamp, Jackson told one observer, "If General Lee wants me, he will send for me." Whatever the reason, Jackson did not impress General Lee during the weeklong series of battles. After it was over, Lee restructured his army, giving General Longstreet command of 28 brigades, while limiting Jackson's command to only seven. Jackson was quick to redeem himself with his stellar performance at Second Manassas. In addition, Lee came to realize that Jackson performed much better in a quasi-independent role and utilized him in that role to great success, whenever possible, until Jackson's death.

Although, in the end, the Seven Days' Battle was a ringing success for the Confederacy because Richmond had been saved, General Lee knew a great opportunity had been missed. "Our success has not been as great or as complete as I could have desired," he wrote to President Davis. "Under ordinary circumstances the Federal Army should have been destroyed." To be fair to Jackson, his men had marched more than 600 miles and fought five battles in the previous few weeks in the Shenandoah Valley before being called to Richmond. Not only did they have to struggle with poor maps and even more poorly marked roads, his Valley men were not used to the heat and humidity of coastal Virginia. Yet their failure to perform at their usual high level cost the Confederacy dearly. According to Major Edward Alexander Porter, an artillerist who would rise to the rank of brigadier general by the end of the war, "We were within reach of military success so great that we might have hoped to end the war with our independence."

Antietam: Spearhead for the Emancipation Proclamation

In September 1862, General Lee, fresh from dismantling General Pope's army at the battle of Second Manassas, decided to go on the attack. For the first time in the war, a Confederate army was going to invade Northern territory. Unfortunately for Lee, things started to go wrong almost immediately. On September 9, 1862, he issued Special Order 191, which split his army into two separate wings—one to head to Harper's Ferry, Virginia (now West Virgina), while the other was to move towards Hagerstown, Maryland. Just days after it had been written, a copy of that order was found by Union soldiers in a field near Frederick, Maryland, giving Union General George McClellan the position and proscribed movements of the entire Army of Northern Virginia. An exultant "Little Mac" proclaimed, "Here is a paper with which if I cannot whip Bobbie Lee, I will be willing to go home."

McClellan did move his army with uncharacteristic zeal and, by September 17, 1862, had Lee's army backed up against the Potomac River near Sharpsburg, Maryland. Here, Lee faced a choice. Either give up and retreat back into Virginia, or stand and fight with his back against an unfordable river. Adding difficulty to Lee's decision was the fact that a third of his army was still 6 miles away in Harper's Ferry. In perhaps his biggest gamble of the war, Lee chose to stay and fight.

Aftermath of the battle of Antietam—still the bloodiest day in American history. (Library of Congress)

Displaying his usual lack of battlefield vigor, McClellan directed the fight from the Pry House, far in the Union rear. Frittering away his huge manpower advantage, McClellan advanced his units in a piecemeal fashion that allowed General Lee to counter each of his attacks. Most puzzling was his lack of attention to General Ambrose Burnside's inability to get his men across Antietam Creek despite facing only token resistance. By the time Burnside's men had broken through and were threatening to break Lee's entire line, General A.P. Hill's men, who had just arrived on the field after marching all the way from Harper's Ferry, crushed the last Union attack of the day.

When the battle was finished, more than 24,000 dead and wounded men lay on the field. It was the bloodiest single day in the Civil War and remains the bloodiest single day in American history. A day after the battle, Lee's army retreated back to Virginia—the invasion was over. An elated McClellan sent news of his "great" victory to President Lincoln: "Maryland is entirely freed from the presence of the enemy, who has been driven across the Potomac." President Lincoln was not so sure that Antietam had been a "great" victory. Lee's Confederate army had been driven from Maryland and had suffered terribly casualties, but it lived to fight another day. To make matters worse, General McClellan looked to be in no hurry to tangle with it again. However, the military victory at Antietam served Lincoln's purpose in another and far more significant way. It gave him the opportunity he had been waiting for—the opportunity to issue the Emancipation Proclamation.

Abraham Lincoln had many reasons for issuing the Emancipation Proclamation, not the least of which was to prevent any possibility of foreign intervention in the war. Both England and France had shown an interest in helping the Confederacy, in exchange for access to the South's primary export—King Cotton. However, with the war dragging on and the casualty list mounting to ever higher proportions, Lincoln came to the realization that the war could no longer be contained as a war to just preserve the Union. This war, if it was to be won, had to be a war for freedom. Lincoln wrote: "The fiery trial through which we pass, will light us down, in honor or dishonor, to the latest generation.... In giving freedom to the slave, we assign freedom to the free—honorable alike in what we give, and what we preserve. We shall nobly save, or meanly lose, the last, best hope of earth."

Atlanta: Gone With the Wind

On May 7, 1864, General William Tecumseh Sherman began playing a perilous game of cat and mouse with his Confederate adversary General Joe Johnston. Sherman had been given orders from General Grant to advance from his base at Chattanooga, Tennessee, and to "engage Johnston's army, to break it up, and to get into the interior of the enemy's country as far as you can, inflicting all the damage you can against their war resources." Sherman's ultimate goal was to capture Atlanta, Georgia, which was probably the most vital supply, manufacturing, and communications center in the Deep South. For two months, Johnston had prevented Sherman from reaching that goal. However, he had also given up hundreds of miles of territory in the process. Emulating Grant, Sherman repeatedly attempted to flank Johnston's carefully prepared defensive positions. Every time his lines were threatened, Johnston would pull back to a new entrenched position somewhere in the rear. Only at Kennesaw Mountain did Sherman attempt to storm Johnston's lines with a frontal assault with disastrous results. However, when Johnston gave up his position along the Chattahoochee River, in the beginning of July, and retired to Peach Tree Creek at the very outskirts of Atlanta, President Jefferson Davis had seen enough.

President Davis was determined to protect Atlanta at all costs. The fall of Atlanta, said Davis, would "open the way for the Federal Army to the Gulf on one hand, and to Charleston on the other." In addition, the city of 20,000 people was home to many of the South's foundries, munitions plants, and supply depots. When his military advisor, Braxton Bragg, suggested replacing the ever-retreating Johnston with General John Bell Hood, who had earned a reputation for fighting in the East, Davis asked General Robert E. Lee's opinion. Despite Lee's response that Hood was "all lion" and "none of the fox," Davis gave him command of the forces guarding Atlanta. It took Hood only three days to launch his first attack. The Confederates were defeated. Hood tried three more times and was badly defeated each time. "This was just what we wanted," said Union commander "Cump" Sherman, "to fight on open ground...instead of being forced to run up against prepared intrenchments."

After losing more than 15,000 men in three days, Hood settled his army into the trenches protecting Atlanta and prepared for a long siege, comfortable in the fact that he still had more than 40,000 men to protect the city. The siege lasted throughout the month of August, until Sherman's men suddenly disappeared. The victory celebration in Atlanta was about to begin, when Hood learned the awful truth. Instead of retreating, Sherman was marching south, to cut the last railroad link to Atlanta in nearby Jonesborough. After a desperate attempt to break the Union hold on his supply line, Hood decided to evacuate Atlanta. The long campaign was over.

General William Tecumseh Sherman, on the outskirts of Atlanta, Georgia. (Library of Congress)

When Sherman wired the news to Washington that "Atlanta is ours, and fairly won," the North erupted in celebration. Cannons roared out 100-gun salutes and newspapers declared that Sherman was the greatest general since Napoleon. When he heard the news, George McClellan, Union ex-general and then Democratic nominee for president, rewrote his acceptance letter. Instead of advocating immediate peace, now "Little Mac" declared that "the Union is the one condition of peace—we ask no more." McClellan needn't have worried about the wording of his letter; Sherman's victory at Atlanta paved the way for Lincoln's overwhelming reelection in November. When the election was over, Lincoln had captured every state except Kentucky, Delaware, and New Jersey, and the Republican party enjoyed a 3/4 majority in Congress. Thanks to Sherman's victory in Atlanta, it was no longer a question of *if* the Union would prevail, but *when* the Union would prevail.

Five Forks: Road to Final Victory

On May 4, 1864, General Ulysses Grant led the Army of the Potomac into Virginia on what would become the last offensive campaign against General Lee's Army of Northern Virginia. After a month of almost constant fighting at places such as Wilderness, Spotsylvania, and Cold Harbor, Grant succeeded in pinning Lee's army into a defensive position. Now Lee's main goal had to be to protect Richmond, the capital of the Confederacy, and Petersburg, the hub of a railroad system that carried food and supplies to the army. Grant pounded away at Lee's lines, to no avail, throughout the long hot summer of 1864. He even gave approval to a risky plan that involved digging a tunnel and placing explosives under the Confederate lines (discussed on page 82, in Chapter 6). Although the resultant explosion created a huge crater, the plan failed, because the breach in the line was quickly sealed and the majority of attacking Union forces became hopelessly trapped.

Grant then turned his attention to extending his lines to the south. Slowly and at great cost, the Union army stretched Lee's lines to the breaking point. But the hungry, tired, and poorly equipped Confederate soldiers were able to turn back every Union assault against their lines. Throughout the fall and winter, both sides settled into a routine in which the Union army would sidle out of the trenches, advance to the south, and face the inevitable Confederate counterattack. If the counterattack was successful, the Union forces would retreat for the day. If it was unsuccessful, both sides would dig in and extend the long lines of trenches that almost surrounded Richmond and Petersburg.

This ugly war of attrition lasted throughout the winter and into the spring of 1865 and showed little signs of changing—until the end of March, when General Phil Sheridan's cavalry, fresh from a raid in northern Virginia, threatened the Southside Railroad by advancing toward Dinwiddie Courthouse. Anticipating the Union maneuver, General Lee sent a 19,000-man force, commanded by General George Pickett, with orders to hold the crossroads town of Five Forks "at all hazards." Pickett's men quickly pushed back the Union advance and settled in to hold the ground should Sheridan organize another attack. Pickett felt his position was so secure that he rode off to join a shad bake being held by fellow Generals Fitzhugh Lee (Robert E. Lee's second oldest son) and Tom Rosser. While the Confederate commanding officer was enjoying his meal, Sheridan's cavalry, reinforced by a corps of Union infantry, launched a devastating attack that quickly shredded Pickett's defenses.

Not only was Five Forks the most one-sided Union victory of the campaign that had begun 11 months earlier, but Union forces had finally cut off access to the Southside Railroad. For months, General Lee had been working on a carefully choreographed plan that would allow his army to link up with Joe Johnston's army operating in North Carolina. Without the Southside Railroad, that plan was no longer feasible. Instead, Lee had to improvise a retreat westward along the Richmond & Danville Railroad—a retreat that would eventually lead his army to Appomattox Court House. While the numbers of men involved in the battle at Five Forks pale in comparison to some of the larger battles in the Civil War, the smashing Union victory there ended the siege and set the stage for the eventual surrender of General Lee and the Army of Northern Virginia.

Confederate prisoners taken after the Union victory at the battle of Five Forks, Virginia. (Library of Congress)

CHAPTER 8

THE MOST INFLUENTIAL CAMPAIGNS OF THE CIVIL WAR

1861, Western Virginia: Lee's First Retreat

In June 1861, two months after Virginia voted to secede, loyal Unionists converged in Wheeling for a convention of their own. Wheeling was a good choice, because voters in northwestern Virginia had overwhelmingly voted against secession. After declaring that the Confederate legislature in Richmond was illegal, the Wheeling Convention elected their own representatives and appointed Francis Pierpont as governor of the state. To provide muscle for this new "government" of Virginia, President Lincoln sent Union forces, commanded by General George McClellan, into western Virginia. In one of the first engagements of the war, McClellan's men scattered a small Confederate force in what became known as the "Phillipi races." After securing the vital Baltimore and Ohio railroad junction at Grafton, McClellan advanced against the remaining Confederate army entrenched on Rich Mountain. Displaying many of the traits he would show later in the war, McClellan split his force and sent a brigade commanded by William Rosecrans over a narrow mountain track to flank the Confederate position. Rosecrans's surprise attack was a complete success, but McClellan, fearing defeat, did not advance, and most of the Confederates were able to escape the trap. Confederate General Robert Garnett was killed a few days later in a rear guard action at Corrick's Ford and became the first general officer to die in the war.

McClellan's victories enabled the Wheeling Convention to reconvene and begin preparations to form a separate state by setting a date in October 1861 for a referendum on the issue. Unwilling to give up such a large section of Virginia without a fight, President Jefferson Davis sent 20,000 reinforcements to western Virginia, along with a new commander—General Robert E. Lee. Lee not only

General Robert E. Lee, commander of the Army of Northern Virginia. (Library of Congress)

hoped to reclaim the lost territory, he also hoped to cut the Baltimore and Ohio Railroad and the Chesapeake and Ohio Canal. This would sever the supply lines connecting Washington to the West and provide an ideal jumping off point for a Confederate advance that could divide the North in half. However, Lee's complicated plan called for the convergence of five separate forces at Cheat Mountain and was foiled by a combination of summer rain, bottomless mud, and difficult terrain. Unable to secure adequate supplies in the barren region, Lee retreated. He tried again in early fall by advancing up the Kanawa Valley. Foiled again by bad weather and seeing little chance of victory, Lee retreated again and was recalled to Richmond. With Union forces now firmly in place, the voters overwhelmingly passed the statehood referendum and a constitutional convention was scheduled. West Virginia was on the verge of becoming the 35th state.

The big loser of the campaign was Robert E. Lee. As soon as he returned to the capital, Lee was assailed as "Granny Lee" and "Evacuating Lee." One paper even went so far as to say he displayed "an extreme tenderness of blood" and that he was "outwitted, outmaneuvered, and outgeneraled." The resounding defeat also reinforced the impression that, at age 54, Lee was only a "desk soldier" who would not have much value on a battlefield. This impression was reinforced when Davis sent Lee to Charleston, South Carolina, to inspect and shore up the seacoast defenses, but at least the Confederacy could benefit from his engineering skills. Lee would not return to command an army in battle until June 1862, when he would once again face off with General George McClellan.

George McClellan was quick to capitalize on his status as the North's first war "hero" when he was first called to Washington and then placed in command of the Union's largest army. McClellan soon convinced President Lincoln to put the elderly General Winfield Scott out to pasture, and at the age of 35, became the commander-in-chief of the entire Union army. In the next few months however, it became glaringly clear that McClellan had been catapulted too quickly to such a high position. Lincoln became increasingly irritated as McClellan refused to commence active operations. Finally McClellan decided, rather than advance forward, to attempt to flank the Confederate line and had the army transported to the York River Peninsula. There, however, he once again hesitated and lost whatever advantage he may have had. When forced to fight against General Lee on relatively equal terms, McClellan was overmatched time and again, until he was ultimately sacked in the fall of 1862.

1862, the Shenandoah Valley: Triumph of Jackson's Foot Cavalry

The Shenandoah Valley posed a unique threat to the war plans of the Union. Its northern terminus, Winchester, was a dagger pointing directly at Washington and was used repeatedly as a jumping off point for offensive operations north of the Mason-Dixon Line, while its southern end gradually led away from the Confederate capital and into Tennessee. It also was home to one of the few macadamized turnpikes in the South, which enabled quick troop movements regardless of weather. In May 1862, Stonewall Jackson was determined to use the geographical features of

the Shenandoah Valley to supplement his small army. Given orders to prevent the Union army, commanded by General Nathaniel Banks, from withdrawing from their position at Winchester and to reinforce General McClellan's drive on Richmond, Jackson launched an attack at nearby Kernstown. Although Jackson was soundly defeated, President Lincoln fell for the bait and ordered Banks and his 50,000 men to remain in Winchester. Jackson, not content to rest on his laurels, then marched his men across the Blue Ridge Mountains, where he faced off against a 25,000-man army commanded by General Nathaniel Fremont. After disrupting Fremont's operations and forcing him to withdraw, Jackson recrossed the Blue Ridge and advanced once again towards Winchester.

In his absence, General Banks had advanced his army to Harrisonburg, but once he realized that Jackson was on the move, Banks ordered a quick retreat to the safety of the forts protecting

General Thomas J. Jackson scored a series of impressive victories in the Shenandoah Valley in 1862. (Library of Congress)

Winchester. However, Jackson's "foot-cavalry," rather than follow in Banks's wake, crossed the Manssanutten Mountain at New Market and surprised the small Union garrison at Front Royal. Although Banks was able to beat Jackson into Winchester, he wasn't prepared when "Old Jack" launched a vicious dawn attack that scattered the Union army. Jackson then continued his advance until he threatened Harper's Ferry. By then, Jackson had the full attention of President Lincoln. All the Federal units that had been earmarked for reinforcing McClellan's army were ordered to march against Jackson. In addition, General Fremont was ordered to cut off the southern end of the Valley, by advancing to Harrisonburg. There were now three separate Union armies, commanded by Generals Fremont, McDowell, and Banks, converging on Jackson's position.

Stonewall Jackson held his army in Winchester until the last possible moment. Then he drove his men hard up the Valley Pike. After narrowly beating a Union division, commanded by General Shields, that intended to cut him off at Strasburg, Jackson made a beeline for the only remaining bridge over the Shenandoah River at Port Republic. However, disaster nearly struck just as Jackson's men reached the small town. A detachment of Federal cavalry swooped in and nearly captured Jackson and his staff, before taking control of the two-lane covered bridge crossing the swollen river. Jackson managed to regroup his scattered army and retake the bridge just before the van of General Fremont's army swung into action against Jackson's rearguard at Cross Keys. The exhausted Jackson allowed General Ewell to fend off Fremont's men as he prepared to cross the river and attack the upcoming elements of General Shields's division. After Ewell succeeded in halting Fremont's advance, Jackson had the remaining portion of his army cross the bridge, before destroying it and leaving Fremont safely on the other side of the unfordable river. The next day, Jackson prevailed once again and forced General Shields to withdraw from the Valley. When Lincoln learned of the twin defeats at Cross Keys and Port Republic, he ordered all three armies to withdraw from the Shenandoah Valley.

In the four-month campaign, Jackson's 17,000-man army had fought and won five out of six battles; confronted three separate Union armies; diverted more than 60,000 men from McClellan's campaign on the Peninsula; captured 9,000 rifles, as well as huge stores of food and medicine; and disrupted two major strategic movements. In the process, Stonewall Jackson became a figure larger than life, in both the North and the South, and helped further the aura of invincibility that the Confederates enjoyed in Virginia. What's more important is that Jackson's improbable string of victories came at a time when enthusiasm for the Confederacy was fading fast. All of Tennessee and most of the Mississippi Valley had fallen, and General McClellan was slowing inching his huge army towards the Confederate capital at Richmond. However, this changed when Jackson joined the next great Confederate military hero, Robert E. Lee, and they combined to defeat McClellan and eventually to bring the war to the North.

1863, Vicksburg Campaign:
The Greatness of Ulysses S. Grant

The last bastion on the Mississippi River held by Confederate forces was Vicksburg, Mississippi. Fortified early in the war, the numerous batteries crowning Vicksburg's 200-foot bluffs negated the advantage held by Union gunboats in the river. General Ulysses S. Grant had been trying to capture the city since December 1862. His first effort failed when Confederate cavalry cut his supply lines at Holly Springs. Grant next decided to descend the river to Milliken's Bend and try to reach Vicksburg via the numerous canals, swampy streams, and bayous of the Yazoo Delta. During the winter of 1862–63, Grant tried four separate approaches to "the Gibraltar of the West" to no avail. He even put his men to work digging a canal that he hoped would cut a new river channel out of reach of Vicksburg's guns. Not only did all these efforts fail, Grant also came very close to losing naval

commander David Dixon Porter's fleet of gunboats, when they became trapped by felled trees. For three long months, Grant tried and failed to find a way to dislodge the defenders of Vicksburg in what one of his officers called "the Valley Forge of the war."

As Grant's troubles mounted, General John Pemberton, the commander of the Confederate forces at Vicksburg, grew increasingly confident and even boasted that "there is no immediate danger here." However, the Pennsylvania-born Pemberton learned he was very wrong on April 11, 1863 when his vaunted river batteries could not stop a squadron of Union gunboats from passing below the city. In all, they fired 525 rounds and scored 68 hits, but were only able to sink one transport ship. With his powerful fleet now below the city, Grant marched

General Ulysses S. Grant led the Union army that captured the Confederate fortress at Vicksburg, Mississippi, in July 1863. (Library of Congress)

his army overland to a position 30 miles south of Vicksburg and prepared to cross to the eastern bank of the Mississippi River. The Vicksburg campaign had begun.

Knowing that he was running out of options, Grant decided to bet all his chips on one roll of the dice. After crossing the river unopposed on April 30, 1863, Grant knew that not only did he no longer have an avenue of retreat, but that he had also cut his own supply line. Confident that his men could live off the land, Grant secured a quick victory at Port Gibson that gave him time to bring reinforcements across the river. Adding to the difficulties Grant faced was the fact that he was opposed by two separate Confederate armies: Pemberton's army in Vicksburg, and General Joe Johnston's army gathering at Jackson, Mississippi. Instead of driving straight for Vicksburg, Grant decided to march east and confront Johnston. After brushing aside a small Confederate force at Raymond, Grant launched a direct assault on Jackson, which scattered Johnston's small army. Leaving General Sherman's division behind to tear up railroad tracks and destroy whatever Confederate stores and armaments were left behind, Grant turned back west towards Vicksburg. Undecided about whether to challenge Grant's army or fall back to the Vicksburg fortifications, Pemberton did neither. Caught flat-footed at Champion's Hill, Pemberton's men were defeated in the largest battle of the campaign. Grant hit them again the next day and captured the last intact bridge across the Big Black River. The road to Vicksburg was now open.

In the 17-day campaign, Grant's army marched 180 miles and fought and won five separate engagements. With Pemberton now locked safely inside his own fort, Sherman admitted to Grant that "until this moment I never thought your expedition a success." After two failed assaults against the city, Grant settled down for a nice old-fashioned siege and six weeks later the city fell. For the Confederacy, Vicksburg was the keystone of the arch and when it collapsed, so did any reasonable hopes for a military victory. While Gettysburg—which ended the day before Grant's signal victory—got more publicity, the fall of Vicksburg divided the Confederacy in two. Not only did it give the Union unfettered access to the Mississippi River, it also showed, once and for all, that the Confederate army could not protect its own territory. With total control of the sea and the length and breadth of the Mississippi, the Union army and navy could now advance into the Confederate heartland from nearly every direction.

1864, the Shenandoah Valley Revisited: Horror in the Valley

In the summer of 1864, with General Grant's grinding offensive inching ever southward, General Lee made perhaps one of his boldest moves of the war. He detached 15,000 men, under the command of Jubal Early, and sent them on a massive raid towards Washington. Using the Shenandoah Valley as a starting point, Early crossed the Potomac River on July 6, 1864. After winning an easy victory three days later at Monocacy, Maryland, Early's men reached the outskirts of Washington on July 11, 1864, and skirmished outside the capital throughout the next day. Although Early was not able to capture Washington, he did force Grant to send an entire corps to defend the city. Early withdrew his men to Winchester, but kept up his harassing tactics until General Grant could no longer ignore him. Turning to one of his boldest generals, Grant gave orders to Phil Sheridan to take command of the Army of the Shenandoah and to follow Early "to the death."

On September 19, 1864, after sparring with Early for a few weeks, General Sheridan launched his campaign by sending two divisions of cavalry, armed with rapid-firing carbines, against Winchester. The ensuing decisive Union victory cost Early a quarter of his men and sent him reeling back up the Shenandoah Valley. Three days later, Sheridan hit Early again at Fisher's Creek, and once again Early's defensive line crumbled. After receiving reinforcements from General Lee, Early sent his cavalry back down the valley to harass the Union army. Given orders by Sheridan to "either whip the enemy or get whipped yourself," cavalry commander Alfred Torbert

General Phil Sheridan led the Union army to victory at the battle of Cedar Creek, Virginia. (Library of Congress)

hit the Rebel horsemen at Tom's Brook and sent them skittering back up the Valley Pike. After having lost three straight battles, Early decided that he needed to change tactics. Despite being outnumbered almost two to one, Early decided to attack the Union camp at Cedar Creek.

As luck would have it, on the date Early chose to attack, Sheridan was en route to Washington for a meeting with Secretary Stanton. Early's surprise dawn assault knocked the leaderless Union army back four miles. However, instead of capitalizing on his success Early let his men break ranks to forage for food from the overrun Union camps. When he heard of the assault, Sheridan immediately turned around and headed back to Cedar Creek. Riding his trusty horse, Rienzi, Sheridan rallied his men and regrouped for a counterattack. One of his men later recalled, "Such a scene as his presence and such emotion as it awoke cannot be realized but once in a century." Using his cavalry once again to lead the attack, Sheridan's men quickly shattered Early's disordered line. In one of the greatest turnarounds of the war, a crippling defeat changed into a glorious victory. With his army virtually wiped out, Early withdrew to Rockfish Gap for the winter. Once spring campaigning began again, General Custer's cavalry regiment wiped out Early's remaining force at Waynesboro. General Early and about 20 others managed to escape, but the once proud army ceased to exist.

While Sheridan's military accomplishments were significant, it was not his only objective in the campaign. Grant had also ordered Sheridan to turn the Shenandoah Valley into a wasteland "so that crows flying over it…have to carry their own provender." Sheridan was as exuberant in this mission as he was in defeating Early. Before he was finished, his men had burned more than 2,000 barns and confiscated in excess of 7,000 cows and sheep. What food couldn't be fed to the troops was destroyed. In the end, 92 miles of the Shenandoah Valley, from Winchester to Staunton, were no longer fit for habitation. In what was the first major campaign to utilize the tools of total war, Grant and Sheridan devastated what had been the breadbasket of the Confederacy, while the people of the Shenandoah Valley were left with nothing except "their eyes with which to weep with over the war."

1865, Appomattox: Final Retreat

On Saturday, April 1, 1865, while worshipping at St. Paul's Church in Richmond, President Jefferson Davis received a telegram from General Lee informing him that the thin gray line protecting the Confederate capital could no longer be held. Davis quietly left the church and was aboard a train headed for Danville, Virginia, that evening. What couldn't be removed was burned, and before long Richmond was awash in flames. General Lee hurried his men across the James River before those bridges were burned as well, and towards Amelia Courthouse, where supplies were waiting and he could be joined by the forces retreating from Petersburg. While Lee was pleased that he had stolen at least a day's march on Grant, Union cavalry units were already nipping at his heals. At Namozine Church, General Custer's men came upon the left flank guard of Lee's column, and in the ensuing skirmish, his adjutant-general and 10 caissons were captured. On the following day, another group of Union cavalry, commanded by Wesley Merritt, almost broke through his lines at Tabernacle Church.

Lee remained confident, and the majority of his men upbeat, during the 40-mile march to Amelia Courthouse, until they discovered that the train cars waiting for them were loaded with ammunition and ordnance equipment instead of food. Lee's army wasted precious hours attempting to forage for food and gave the Union infantry time to cut their escape route at Burkeville. Lacking alternatives, Lee continued the westward march towards Farmville, the next train station where he could receive rations for his half-starved men. Disaster struck Lee's army again at Saylor's Creek. While General Lee was busy directing the head of the column, Union cavalry led by General Custer sliced off a quarter of his remaining men that were stuck behind a long train of wagons. When the shaken Lee learned what had happened, he exclaimed: "My god, has the army been dissolved?"

At long last, Lee was able to secure rations at Farmville on April 7, 1865. However, before he could savor this small triumph, word came that Union troops had also crossed the Appomattox River at nearby High Bridge and were closing fast.

After detailing his remaining cavalry to fend off the Union advance, Lee continued the westward march towards Appomattox Station. With fewer than 15,000
troops remaining in the once proud Army of Northern Virginia, Lee's weary men
went into camp a few miles east of Appomattox Court House. Unbeknownst to
them, their commander had been exchanging a series of letters, for the previous
several days, with General Grant on possible surrender terms. Lee ordered one
last assault early the next morning in the hopes of dislodging the Union cavalry that
had been prowling around Appomattox Station. At first the assault went well and it
looked like the way was clear for the army to escape once again. But then Union
infantry began to arrive. When they formed for attack, the line of blue-coated
soldiers stretched 3 miles, and when the overwhelming attack came, Lee's escape
route was finally closed. Said Lee, "There is nothing left me to do but go and see
General Grant, and I would rather die a thousand deaths."

While Lee's conduct in this last heartbreaking campaign was exemplary as usual,
it was his decision to surrender his army rather than disband it that was perhaps the
most graceful decision of his military career. Letting his men go, Lee feared, would
turn them into lawless guerrillas and marauders. According to Lee: "The enemy's
cavalry would pursue them and overrun many sections they may never [otherwise]
have occasion to visit. We would bring on a state of affairs it would take the country
years to recover from." In his final act as commander of the army, Lee met with
Grant on April 9, 1865 and secured as favorable terms as he could have hoped. He
then retired from the army. For Lee and his men, the war was over, and in a few
short weeks, it would be over for the rest of the Confederacy.

General Lee surrenders to General Grant at Appomattox Court House.
(Library of Congress)

CHAPTER 9

MYSTERIES OF
THE DEEP

Submarine Warfare:
Early Attempts, Failures, and Death

The first working submarine, a wooden rowboat covered with waterproof hides, was invented by a Dutch scientist named Cornelius van Drebbel in 1620. More than 150 years later, David Bushnell designed the first submarine adapted for military purposes. Bushnell, a 29-year-old student at Yale University, got the idea from a story published in the *English Gentleman's Magazine*. He called the vessel *Turtle* because it was made from two hollowed-out wooden slabs that looked like turtle shells. The *Turtle* failed in its only attempt to sink the British warship HMS *Eagle* lying at anchor in the New York harbor, when the torpedo could not be properly attached. The *Turtle* was eventually sunk, along with the sloop that was carrying her, when Bushnell tried to smuggle the small vessel out of New York City. Robert Fulton, a close friend of one of Bushnell's classmates, built a scaled-up, bronze-covered version of the *Turtle* and tried to sell it to Napoleon in 1800, but the French navy wasn't interested. Fulton then tried to sell his invention to the British government but eventually gave up on the idea and turned his attention to steamboats. Early in 1861 Julius Kroehl, an engineer for the Pacific Pearl Company, was the first inventor to come forward during the Civil War with plans for a working submarine. Kroehl's cigar-shaped vessel was designed to enter enemy harbors and clear out underwater obstructions. The design was rejected by the Union navy, but Kroehl continued to build the vessel in New York harbor with private funds. Construction of the *Explorer* was completed in the summer of

1864 and Kroehl sent a letter and pamphlet explaining the design of the ship to President Jefferson Davis of the Confederacy. The *Explorer* carried large quantities of compressed air, which equalized pressure in the vessel and allowed the bottom of the boat to open and close for underwater divers. The design was forwarded to the Secretary of the Navy and then to the Chief Naval Engineer, but the Confederate navy also passed on Kroehl's invention. Unable to sell his submarine, Kroehl had the *Explorer* towed to the Pearl Islands near the Bay of Panama, where she was finally put to use harvesting pearl-bearing oysters.

One of the first inventors to approach President Jefferson Davis with a submarine design was William Cheeney, an engineer who worked for the Navy Department in Richmond, Virginia. Cheeney's two-man submarine was designed to carry an underwater diver who rode in a small compartment in the bow. While the vessel was submerged, the diver would attach an explosive device to the bottom of an enemy ship and then return to the submarine. The vessel was launched in the James River in the fall of 1861. It was then taken to Hampton Roads where a correspondent from the *New York Herald* documented her attempt to sink the USS *Minnesota*: "On Wednesday evening…an infernal machine (submarine) was sent down from Seawall's Point for the purpose of blowing up the flag-ship. She came down to the ship without difficulty, but she caught in the grappling…hanging from the jib-boom of the ship." According to the correspondent, the vessel was "built of iron" and "ballasted by means of water, let in and forced

out by means of a pump." The ultimate fate of this submarine is unknown. On March 13, 1862, Cheeney took delivery of a newly modified submarine from the Tredegar Iron Works in Richmond, which was probably equipped with the first "submarine cannon." This submarine has also disappeared without a trace and without any evidence that it was ever operational during the war. In all likelihood, Cheeney's submarine experiments in the James River were scrapped in May 1862 when the river entrance was sealed off by obstructions designed to prevent Union gunboats from attacking Richmond. Unable to continue his work, Cheeney deserted in the fall of 1862 and eventually wound up opening a lead smelting business in Missouri.

Drawing by Alfred Waud, depicting Confederate underwater torpedoes that spurred Union research into submarines. (Library of Congress)

Inventors in other Southern cities were also working on submarine designs early in the war. In Savannah, Georgia, Charles Wilkinson and Charlie Carroll finished their work on a small submarine early in 1862. They launched it in the Savannah harbor on February 23, 1862, but discovered one of the air valves did not work properly. Carroll escaped the sinking vessel, but Wilkinson became the first submariner to die in the war when he drowned before anyone could rescue him.

Similar submarine projects were going on in various other locations around that time, as well. In Mobile, Alabama, a small "submarine apparatus" of unknown origin, was "boarded and sunk" on January 5, 1862. Nothing else is known about this mysterious vessel. New Orleans was also a hotbed of submarine building activity. Today, there is a small submarine on display at the Louisiana State Museum that was discovered by a dredge boat in 1879. The vessel has a "sharp iron prow" designed to puncture the bottom of an enemy ship, but not much is known except that it was probably constructed by the same group that later built the iron ram CSS *Manassas*. Five submarines were also built late in the war in the Department of the Trans-Mississippi. These 40-foot-long iron vessels were all built from the same design and were propelled by a hand crank. One was built in Houston, Texas, and the other four were constructed in Shreveport, Louisiana. All five were scuttled when the war ended and have never been recovered.

One of the buildings in Mobile, Alabama, where submarines were constructed. (Official Naval Records)

In the Brooklyn Navy Yard, Major Edward B. Hunt of the Army Corps of Engineers developed a one-man submarine that was ready for testing in the fall of 1863. Although Hunt's activities were supposed to be secret, the *New York Times* printed a large story about him, stating, "For many months...[Hunt] was engaged in the construction of the fortifications of Key West, Florida. Sometime after his return North he commenced devoting himself to the modeling of his submarine." Unfortunately, Hunt's project was abandoned when he died three days after taking the boat under the water for a test dive on October 30, 1863. According to a naval doctor, Hunt "died of the effects of the respiration of Mephitic air (air lacking oxygen)." Hunt, the first Union submarine fatality of the Civil War, left behind a widow and an 8-year-old son.

In early 1864, Confederate engineer John P. Halligan was granted an exemption from service in the Confederate military to work on a submarine of his own design in Selma, Alabama. On June 16, 1864, Halligan announced that the submarine would be ready for launch in a few days. The interesting thing about Halligan's submarine, named the *Saint Patrick*, was that it was equipped with a small steam engine for propulsion when it was on the surface and a hand crank when it was under the water. However, after four months of unproductive testing in Mobile Bay, the Confederate War Department became impatient with the Irish-born inventor. According to General Dabney Maurey, "Halligan...has not yet used his torpedo boat [and] I do not believe he ever will." Finally, on January 24, 1865, the Naval Department authorized the appropriation of the *Saint Patrick* and ordered Lieutenant John Walker to take command of the vessel. Three nights later, Walker took the submarine on her first combat mission. Shortly after midnight, an attack was made against the USS *Octorara*, a 10-gun paddle-wheel steamboat, but the torpedo, which lodged near her wheelhouse, misfired. Several shots were fired at the CSS *Saint Patrick*, but Walker and the submarine escaped unharmed. There is no record of the CSS *Saint Patrick* making any more sorties against the Union fleet after that, and it is likely that the ship was used to run the blockade and ferry supplies to the garrison at Spanish Fort before being scuttled when the Union army captured Mobile on April 12, 1865.

Union Submariners:
An Alligator in the James River

On May 16, 1861, the Philadelphia harbor police spotted a strange vessel traveling down the Delaware River near the Philadelphia Naval Yard. The crew of four was arrested when it was discovered that the vessel was a submarine. The inventor of this remarkable boat was a French mathematician named Brutus de Villeroi, who had already built a submarine in France that was used for salvage operations. De Villeroi's latest creation was intended to be used to recover gold from a Dutch ship that had sunk in the Delaware River during the Revolutionary War. Captain DuPont, the commandant of the Philadelphia Navy Yard, examined the vessel and recommended that de Villeroi be hired to build a similar vessel for the navy. On November 1, 1861, de Villeroi agreed to a contract that specified the construction of one iron submarine for $14,000. After considerable delays and squabbling over the cost of expensive chemicals de Villeroi wanted for the ship's air-scrubbing system, the ship was launched on May 2, 1862. After testing the 40-foot submarine for a month and a half, the ship was given a new commander—Samuel Eakins—and a new coat of green paint and was ordered into action in Hampton Roads, Virginia. After being towed to City Point, Virginia, the submarine, dubbed the USS *Alligator*, was ready for its first mission. It had been hoped the *Alligator* would be ready in time to confront the new Confederate ironclad, CSS *Virginia*. However, after the navy yard at Norfolk, Virginia, was captured by Union forces and the CSS *Virginia* was scuttled, the USS *Alligator* was given a new target: the Petersburg railroad bridge over the Appomattox River. This target also became impracticable when the Union army retreated from the James River Peninsula and the USS *Alligator* was towed back to Philadelphia.

Lieutenant Selfridge was then given command of the vessel, but was relieved after giving an unflattering report of the *Alligator's* propulsion system. Although de Villeroi's first vessel used a screw propeller, the USS *Alligator* was equipped with a set of oars that proved almost completely ineffective. In the winter of 1862–63, it was refitted with a manually driven screw propeller that doubled her speed to four knots. After a series of test dives in March 1863, the USS *Alligator*, once again being captained by Acting Master Eakins, was deemed operational and ordered to report to Charleston, South Carolina. The plan this time was for the *Alligator* to remove the mines in Charleston harbor protecting Fort Sumter, in preparation for an all-out naval assault on the Confederate stronghold. On March 31, 1863 the submarine began its voyage, tethered to the steamer *Philadelphia*. Just as the two ships were passing Cape Hatteras, they were struck by a fierce storm with gale force winds. After struggling for more than eight hours to keep both vessels afloat, the captain of the *Philadelphia* was forced to cut the submarine adrift to save his own ship, later reporting, "I gave the order at 6 p.m. and the ship instantly surged again and cleared a very high and heavy sea." Five days after the USS *Alligator* was lost at sea, the naval attack on Fort Sumter failed, in part because of the large number of underwater mines in Charleston Harbor.

The Union navy continued to experiment with submarines for the rest of the war. The most ambitious project was carried out in Newark, New Jersey, by a firm called the American Submarine Company. However, cost overruns and construction delays kept the new submarine, named the *Intelligent Whale*, in dry dock until after the war. It was finally launched in April 1866 and proved to be a complete disaster. As many as 30 men were killed in sea trials before the *Intelligent Whale* was dry docked forever. This failure put an end to any further American submarine experiments for the next 30 years. Brutus de Villeroi's invention did live on in a slightly different format. Four years after the Civil War ended, Jules Verne published *20,000 Leagues Under the Sea*. Verne, like de Villeroi, was a native of Nantes, France, and probably based his fictional submarine on the designs of his countryman. There are also numerous other historical references in Verne's novel. Captain Nemo's submarine was named the *Nautilus*, after Samuel Fulton's early submarine, and he was chased throughout the book by the USS *Abraham Lincoln*, the captain of which was named after Admiral David Farragut—the hero of the naval battles at New Orleans and Mobile Bay.

The Union submarine named the Intelligent Whale *wasn't finished until the war ended. (Official Naval Records)*

Success at Last:
Adventures of the Singer Submarine Corps

The first submarine privateer was built in New Orleans by two steam gauge manufacturers named James McClintock and Baxter Watson. The 34-foot keel was laid in the fall of 1861 at the Leeds Foundry. On March 12, 1862 the three-man submarine, named *Pioneer*, was ready for launching. At some point during the construction, McClintock and Watson were joined by a wealthy lawyer and an assistant customs agent named Horace Hunley. The small submarine was tested in Lake Pontchartain and was found to be able to stay submerged for two hours at a time. On March 31, 1862, the owners were granted letters of marque from the Confederate government, which gave them a license to sink Union ships for reward money. It is not known if the *Pioneer* was ever deployed, but there is evidence that two men were killed while conducting test dives in Lake Pontchartain. The *Pioneer* was scuttled in the New Basin Canal when New Orleans was captured by Union forces in April 1862. After the war the *Pioneer* was recovered and sold as scrap metal for $43 in 1868.

McClintock, Watson, and Hunley began work on a second, larger submarine in Mobile, Alabama, in May 1862. In an effort to create a more efficient propulsion system, the Confederate inventors concentrated their efforts on building an "electro-magnetic" engine. According to McClintock, this effort wasted "much time and money." Baxter Watson even offered to travel to New York City to purchase an electric engine if the Confederate government agreed to pay the $5,000 cost.

Unable to build an engine that would generate enough power to be useful, the inventors focused their efforts on building a compact steam engine that could power the submarine. By January 1863, they were forced to acknowledge defeat in this endeavor as well and equipped the *Pioneer II* with a hand-cranked propulsion system. The five-man submarine was launched in Mobile Bay later in the month, but was lost when it sank in heavy seas while being towed near Fort Morgan.

The loss of the *Pioneer II* was especially hard on Horace Hunley who had been the sole investor in the submarine. When McClintock, Watson, and Hunley began work on a new submarine, they sought outside investors to share the expenses. In April 1863, a group of five investors who had already contracted to build underwater mines for Mobile Bay agreed to put up two-thirds of the $15,000 needed to construct the submarine. The remaining $5,000 was paid by Hunley. The group named themselves the Singer Submarine Corps, and work was begun immediately. The new vessel, which had a 40-foot keel and room for an eight-man crew, was even bigger than the *Pioneer II*. The *H.L. Hunley* was completed and ready for harbor trials by the end of July 1863. Brigadier General James Slaughter, commander of the Mobile defenses, witnessed several of the *H.L. Hunley's* early trials. "I saw her pass under a large raft of lumber towing a torpedo behind her which destroyed the raft. She appeared three or four hundred yards beyond the raft and so far as I could judge she behaved as well under water as above it." When it was decided that the water in Mobile harbor was too shallow for safe operations, the *H.L. Hunley* was offered to General Beauregard for use in Charleston Harbor.

General Beauregard, commander of the defenses at Charleston, South Carolina, accepted the offer and the submarine was loaded on a railroad car on August 7, 1863. The *H.L. Hunley* arrived four days later and immediately began testing in the harbor. As an incentive, a private company in Charleston offered a reward of $100,000 if the *H.L. Hunley* was able to sink the ironclad USS *Ironsides* and $50,000 for every monitor that it could sink. By the end of August the submarine had made three unsuccessful forays into the harbor in search of a Union vessel, but the stakes were suddenly raised when the Union army began bombarding the city. Anxious to retaliate, the Singer Submarine Corps was promised $27,500 by the Confederate government, and the navy was given permission to appropriate the vessel (adding the Confederate naval prefix CSS to the name). Lieutenant John Payne was made the new commander of the submarine, and a crew of sailors was drafted from the CSS *Chicora*. On August 29, 1863, Payne took the CSS *H.L. Hunley* into the harbor to practice diving. On its return to the dock, the submarine suddenly submerged without warning. Only Payne and one crew member were able to escape before the submarine sank to the bottom. The ship was recovered several weeks later, and Horace Hunley volunteered to take command of the vessel. Hunley recruited Lieutenant Dixon of the 21st Alabama Infantry to captain the submarine, and Dixon engaged in weeks of successful testing. However, on October 15, 1863, when

Dixon was out of town, Hunley decided to take the boat out himself. The result was a disaster. While diving under the CSS *Indian Chief*, the submarine never resurfaced. When the CSS *H.L. Hunley* was recovered again in early November, it was determined that the crew had died of asphyxiation after Hunley had forgotten to close the sea cock and water had flooded into the submarine.

THE C.S.S. HUNLEY

The little submarine was covered with tarpaulins and secretly transported from Mobile to Charleston. Photo reproduced from the collection of the U.S. Library of Congress.

Too long to fit on a standard 20' flat car, the "Hunley" was cradled and tied down on two flatcars for her trip from Mobile. Drawing adapted by C. King from sketch of Hunley by Caldwell C. Whistler and stock art of engine, coal car, and flatcars.

The submarine CSS H.L. Hunley, *being transported to Charleston, South Carolina. (Library of Congress)*

Although General Beauregard had grave doubts about letting the CSS *Hunley* back into the water, Lieutenant Dixon finally convinced him to give it one last chance. Despite the previous tragedies, Dixon had no trouble recruiting a new crew for the vessel. After a series of trials in shallow water, Beauregard ordered Dixon to take the *Hunley* into action on December 14, 1863. However, Dixon found that the ship could not safely tow a torpedo in the rough waters outside the harbor. To solve this problem, Dixon fitted the boat with a spar and attached the torpedo to the front of the submarine. Once the torpedo was driven into the side of an enemy vessel, it was to back away to a safe distance and detonate it with a lanyard. But Dixon's job was made even more difficult when two Confederate sailors deserted and brought news to the Union navy that a submarine was operating in Charleston Bay. When the Union vessels operating closest to the city were fitted with special chain booms, Dixon decided to go after the wooden ships anchored farther out. After several unsuccessful voyages, Dixon and the CSS *H.L. Hunley* set out again on February 17, 1864. Shortly after 8 p.m., Dixon spotted the USS

Housatonic and prepared to make his run. The submarine was spotted by Union lookouts when it got within 100 yards, but the officer on deck thought it was a porpoise and didn't beat to quarters until it was too late. As the *Hunley* slowly backed away, the torpedo exploded and ripped a huge gash in the side of the Union vessel, which sank almost immediately. Fortunately for the crew, the *Housatonic* was anchored in very shallow water and the survivors were able to scramble up the rigging until help could arrive. The crew of the CSS *Hunley* was not so lucky. The submarine survived the explosion and was on her way back to shore when she surfaced and exchanged signals with lookouts posted on Battery Marshal. At some point after that, however, the submarine disappeared beneath the waves with her entire crew.

The wreck of the CSS *H.L. Hunley* was discovered in 1995 by a diving expedition and, on August 8, 2000, she was raised to the surface and transported to a specially built laboratory near the old Charleston Navy Shipyard. The remains of the eight crewmen were recovered and buried with military honors at the Charleston Magnolia Cemetery. Of the approximately 200 submarines that were either designed or built during the Civil War, the *Hunley* was the only one to successfully sink an enemy warship.

Although submarine experimentation ended in the United States shortly after the war, Europe was "ablaze with submarine fever." Ironically, the last European country to develop its own submarine design was Germany, which didn't build a functional unterseeboot until 1905. Nine years later—and 50 years after the CSS *H.L. Hunley* sunk the USS *Housatonic*—the German *U-21* became the second submarine to sink an enemy warship when she fired a single torpedo at the HMS *Pathfinder* in the North Sea near the Orkney Islands, and the British light cruiser went down when the ship's magazine exploded. The world only had to wait nine days for the next submarine to strike. This time it was England's *E-9*, which sank a German cruiser 6 miles south of Heligoland. The golden age of submarines had begun.

Wreckage of the German U-20 *that sunk the Lusitania and sister ship of the* U-21—*the first submarine to sink an enemy vessel in 50 years. (Library of Congress)*

PART FOUR

THE MEDICINE

Doctors and surgeons of the Civil War era were part of the last generation of medical practitioners to operate in what some call the "Dark Ages of Medicine." When President Lincoln was shot, one of the first doctors on the scene probed the wound by thrusting his unwashed finger into the bullet hole. By so doing, he all but guaranteed that Lincoln would never recover from his injuries. If the bullet wound itself hadn't been fatal, infection would have surely set in and Lincoln would have joined the thousands of men who died as a result of misguided medical care. In fact, the harsh treatment wounded soldiers received meant that most who survived did so despite the medical treatment they received, rather than because of it. This section examines several issues and practices of Civil War doctors and surgeons and how their lack of basic medical information hampered their effectiveness. In addition, the treatment received and the medical ailments of a number of generals will be analyzed.

CHAPTER 10

THE WORST DOCTORS IN THE UNION ARMY

Eating Disorders and the Hospital Fund

More than 600,000 soldiers died while serving in the military during the Civil War. The vast majority of these men died *not* on the battlefield but as a result of an illness contracted while in the army. Men from the Midwest who joined the Union army were hit particularly hard, dying from disease at a rate 43 percent higher than the rest of the army. With this much sickness, disease, and death, the 12,000 Union doctors—and their 3,500 Confederate counterparts—had their hands full even when the two armies weren't locked in mortal combat. However, treating sick men was only one of a myriad of tasks assigned to doctors and surgeons during the Civil War. As an officer (a surgeon would be given the rank of major while an assistant surgeon would usually be a captain), every doctor was also responsible for procuring his own food supply, and if a doctor ever ate food intended for enlisted men or for hospital patients, he was guilty of violating Article 39 of the *Articles of War and Regulations of the Army,* which was punishable with a dishonorable discharge from the army. For line officers, this eating arrangement was a minor inconvenience as they typically pooled their money and formed messes. However, the medical staff of a regiment on the march would typically consist of two officers (the surgeon and assistant surgeon) and a small staff of enlisted men (hospital stewards and nurses). Because the surgeon and assistant surgeon were the only officers, they had to buy and eat their food separately from their staff and patients, who could draw their rations from the regimental quartermaster.

The other major food-related issue that a doctor had to deal with was something called the "hospital fund." The hospital fund came about because it was assumed by the army that a sick man needed less food than a healthy man. The hospital drew rations for sick men, which cost the army 13 cents apiece, while rations for a healthy soldier cost the Union army 30 cents per meal. The 17-cent difference between the two were expected to be tabulated by the surgeon-in-charge and made up the hospital fund, which could be used to buy "delicacies, when obtainable." These delicacies were usually such things as fresh vegetables, butter, and milk. However, if these items were unavailable, as they often were, the money could be diverted to other uses. Thus, a sick or wounded patient in a Union army hospital could expect to have his rations cut at a time when his body desperately needed extra nutrients and had to rely upon army doctors to utilize the "saved" money to purchase "delicacies" that could mean the difference between life and death. By 1863 even Surgeon General William Hammond realized that the hospital fund could not "support a proper diet for the sick." However, Hammond didn't put an end to the practice; he only ordered that hospital fund money could not be diverted from its intended purpose.

Union Zouaves practice putting injured soldiers into an ambulance early in the war. (Library of Congress)

Edward Boemer:
Misapplication of Stores and Money

One Union surgeon who ran afoul of the arcane regulations regarding the hospital fund was Dr. Edward Boemer, the regimental surgeon for the Fourth Missouri Infantry. This mostly German regiment was stationed near Pacific City, Missouri, during the summer of 1862. During that time the rations offered to

Boemer's hospital patients were as follows: "Breakfast—coffee, bread and the quarter-ration men, water soup. Dinner—beef soup, and the quarter-ration men, water soup. Supper—tea or coffee, bread and molasses, sometimes butter, and the quarter-ration men, water soup again."

The specific charges against Dr. Boemer were that he "boarded himself on hospital stores" and that he charged money from several of his patients for extra food while they were in the hospital. One of these patients, Lieutenant Henry German, was billed 30 cents a day and another, Lieutenant Lewis Miller, paid $18 for food during the nine weeks he was a hospital patient. Boemer was brought up on charges based on the testimony of a hospital nurse who said that Boemer "had chicken and eggs more than the rest of the men" and the regimental quartermaster who said that Boemer had not accounted for any of the money he received from his patients. Although Boemer submitted pages of explanations for his behavior and attempted to rebut every charge against him, he was found guilty and dismissed from service in the Union Army.

Enoch Blanchard:
The Case of the Illegal Sweet Potatoes

Assistant surgeon Enoch Blanchard was the acting regimental surgeon for the Seventh Vermont Infantry while it was stationed in Pensacola, Florida, in late 1862. During his tenure, Blanchard lost more than 400 men to disease and contracted malaria himself. In an effort to provide a better diet for the men in the New England regiment who were suffering from the hostile climate, Blanchard created a plan for charging the doctors to eat at the hospital, which was approved by the regimental commander Colonel William Holbrook. However, that did not prevent Blanchard from being court-martialed for appropriating "potatoes and other vegetables and provisions" purchased with money from the hospital fund. At issue, specifically, were some sweet potatoes purchased in New Orleans that had been carried into Blanchard's quarters.

Private George Wardwell, a hospital cook, testified that the sweet potatoes drawn from the doctor's quarters were "not enough to pay for what [the doctor] drew from the hospital cook room." But Wardwell also stated that "Dr. Blanchard took money out of his own pocket…to buy extras for the sick." Jacob Dodge, another cook, stated that the hospital "never had so many provisions as when Dr. Blanchard was in charge." The hospital wardmaster explained that the doctors were charged 50 cents a day when they ate at the hospital and that the money was used for purchasing extra food. "Before we lived on salt junk. If we wanted extras we had to purchase them ourselves. Now we have potatoes, onions, butter, and milk nearly all the time." When the court reached a verdict they found Blanchard not guilty. However, they did censure him for taking provisions from the hospital and "especially for not keeping an accurate account of the hospital fund."

Alonza Eisenlord: Innocent of All Charges

Dr. Alonza Eisenlord had been a practicing physician since 1844 before he volunteered to be the surgeon of the Seventh New York Infantry shortly after the war started. He was court-martialed for the first time for stealing two dollars found in a bureau drawer in a farmhouse being used as a hospital near Fortress Monroe, Virginia. Although Eisenlord protested, citing that he had reported the incident, the regimental commander Colonel John Bendix testified that Eisenlord had only done so after he had been reported for the theft. After the trial Eisenlord was found guilty and dismissed from the service. The sentence was approved by Major General John Wool, but Eisenlord was reinstated for unknown reasons by President Lincoln and returned to the regiment in January 1862. The officers were so unhappy to have him back that 22 of them signed a petition asking that he be sent to a different regiment. Their request was denied.

Before the month was over, Dr. Eisenlord found himself court-martialed for a second time. This time the charge was that he had misapplied "food and supplies sent by a civilian relief agency" during the previous summer. The relief agency in question was the New York Union Defense Committee, which had sent boxes of canned meat, wine, and cheese to the regimental hospital. Captain Edward Becker, the regimental quartermaster, testified that he had given an invoice for the articles in question to Eisenlord and that the items had been stored in the doctor's tent. During the time that Eisenlord had possession of these items, the hospital cook testified that he had only salt pork and salt beef to feed the sick men in the hospital. Henry Doell, a hospital nurse, testified that Eisenlord did send rice, coffee, and crackers to the hospital but that they were spoiled. When the doctor's tent was searched, it was found to contain all sorts of boxes from the Union Defense Committee. According to Doell's testimony, "Some boxes were empty and some had been cut round with a knife.... Some had labels on them such as peaches and apples, other boxes had rice, coffee, and sugar all mixed together. There was a loaf of sugar half eaten by rats [and] a loaf of cheese [that] was rotten."

To make matters worse for Dr. Eisenlord, the hospital steward testified that whenever he asked the doctor for sheets or medicine Eisenlord said that there was none and that, "Although the doctor always told us he had no supplies, we found two syringes, a bundle of flax, two boxes of lint, four dozen

Chaotic scene outside a field hospital after a battle. (Library of Congress)

bandages, two double wool blankets, four pillows, a dozen drawers, eighteen gowns, six shirts, two loaves of sugar, five pounds of tea…, two bottles of pickles, two bottles of port wine, one bottle of dark brandy, one bottle of bourbon whisky, and two boxes of solidified milk." Despite the fact that two other witnesses gave almost identical testimony, Eisenlord was found innocent of all charges. The only explanation for the doctor's bizarre behavior was that he felt he had been "treated rudely" during the first court-martial. Dr. Eisenlord complained that the quarter-master refused to assign him living quarters and that he had been forbidden from entering the hospital. It was during the time that the doctor was not allowed to see patients that he began hoarding supplies in his tent. The Seventh New York didn't have to put up with Dr. Eisenlord for much longer, however; he contracted malaria and resigned from the service in August 1862.

Drunken Doctors in Operation

The doctors on the popular television program M*A*S*H had to build their own still to get enough alcohol to drink. Such was not the case for doctors operating during the Civil War. Alcohol was considered to have stimulating medicinal properties and was kept on hand in liberal quantities whenever possible. Alcohol was used on a regular basis as a treatment for infection, malaria (with quinine), pneumonia, and to ease the suffering of patients awaiting surgery. As an ordinary part of his general administrative duties, a Civil War doctor would be responsible for procuring and storing alcohol, as well as prescribing it when necessary. As a result, a doctor or surgeon who had a fondness for alcohol would have almost unlimited access to it while going about his official duties. Thus, it shouldn't be a surprise that 18 percent of all court-martial cases involving doctors mention alcohol in one form or another. The problem of alcoholic doctors was exacerbated by the fact that there was no sure way of determining if a doctor was under the influence while on duty. When line officers were unhappy with how their wounded comrades were being treated, as was often the case, accusations that the doctor was drunk were often filed. These cases usually ended poorly for the doctor in question as courts tended to believe the testimony of line officers and men over the testimony of doctors and other medical staff. And, as there was usually no definitive proof one way or the other, the doctor in question was often found guilty and discharged from the service as a result.

Luther G. Thomas: Drunk on Duty

A graduate of Princeton University and the College of Physicians and Surgeons in New York, Dr. Thomas had practiced medicine for 10 years before volunteering to become the surgeon for the 26th New Jersey Infantry in 1861. Three months into his tenure, during the battle of Fredericksburg, Thomas was ordered to establish a divisional hospital at White Oak Church. Thomas was hampered by the fact that he spent several hours arguing with Provost-Martial Lieutenant Charles Eccelston about the use of a nearby horse stable for wounded patients. Eccelston insisted that he needed the stable for his horse and instructed the sentry to "shoot the doctor if he took my horse out of the stable." In the end, Dr. Thomas did not get use of the stable and, as a result, several men had to lay by the road while waiting for space in the hospital. Eccelston also testified at Thomas's court-martial that he believed Thomas was drunk because he "talked thick as if his tongue were edgewise in his mouth."

Lieutenant Anthony Davis seconded Eccelston's testimony. "Dr. Thomas appeared as if he had been taking ardent spirits." Davis also noted that Thomas fell off his horse and seemed incapable of riding or talking straight. Private William Wyatt was also an eyewitness to Dr. Thomas's fall from his horse, although he also noted that the ground was wet and slippery. Perhaps the most damning testimony came from Captain James McNair who complained that four of his men froze to death "for want of shelter" and that several men crawled off into the woods and built "bough shelters" in an attempt to keep warm. Dr. Thomas presented eight witnesses, all hospital workers, on his behalf who testified that he had not been drunk during the time in question. Private Ezekial Emerson, a hospital nurse, testified that there were only 11 deaths at the hospital: "nine from typhoid and two from inflammation of the spine." In addition, Emerson was certain that no patients had frozen to death. When Dr. Thomas testified,

The White Oak Church building, used as a hospital after the battle of Fredericksburg. (Library of Congress)

he stated that, from December 10 to December 18, the hospital had treated an average of 250 patients a day, with a one-day maximum of 320 patients. During that time, according to Thomas, there were only six deaths, which were all from disease. Despite the evidence provided by Thomas, he was found guilty and ordered to be relived of duty. The reviewing general disapproved the sentence and Thomas was eventually restored to duty. He was mustered out of the service in June 1863 and died in 1864, possibly as a result of contracting hepatitis while in the army.

William H. Lakeman:
Never Mix Brandy and Opium

A native of London, England, Dr. William Lakeman claimed to be a graduate of the esteemed St. Thomas Medical and Surgical College. Despite his shaky credentials, Dr. Lakeman began the war as a private in the 13th New York Infantry, in 1861, but quickly got himself promoted to hospital steward and then to assistant surgeon. He was court-martialed twice in 1862 for being drunk while on duty. The first time, Dr. Lakeman was charged with neglecting his patients during a four-week drinking spree, but he was acquitted. The second time, he was charged with giving the wrong medicine to his patients while intoxicated. This time Lakeman was found guilty and dismissed from the army. However, within eight months he was serving as the assistant surgeon for the 76th New York Infantry and was again court-martialed on October 27, 1862 for being drunk while on duty at Crampton's Gap the previous month. As with the case involving Dr. Luther Thomas, there was conflicting testimony about Dr. Lakeman's condition. Major Charles Livingston testified that, although Dr. Lakeman wasn't "decidedly drunk," he was under the influence of liquor. Lieutenant Jacob Chur, the acting assistant adjutant general, testified that he could tell Dr. Lakeman was intoxicated, at a distance of 20 yards, from "his manner and his gait."

Lieutenant James Godard saw Dr. Lakeman take several drinks from his flask of brandy during the day and admitted to taking a drink from the doctor's flask himself, but testified that the doctor did not "look intoxicated." Dr. Lakeman did not deny drinking brandy and also admitted to taking several doses of opium to treat his own acute dysentery. Dr. Lakeman testified that he had consulted with another doctor who had advised him to take the opium. In an effort to prove that he had not been intoxicated, Lakeman called upon his aide to testify that he had been able to attend to his horse. Despite the fact that Dr. Lakeman was capable of taking the saddle off his horse, he was found guilty of all charges and, once again, dismissed from the army. But Dr. Lakeman's battle with the bottle, as well as the U.S. military, did not end there. While in Washington, two years later, he was again arrested by the military and charged with drunkenness. This time Dr. Lakeman ended up spending time in the Old Capital Prison for being in the city "without proper authority."

Wounded soldiers waiting for medical treatment after a battle. (Library of Congress)

William B. Hezlep:
Never Too Drunk to Operate

A graduate of Jefferson Medical College in Philadelphia, Pennsylvania, Dr. Hezlop had spent two years as the surgeon for the Third Pennsylvania Cavalry before he was court-martialed in February 1864. The specific charge was that he had been intoxicated while treating injured patients from the battle of New Hope Church during the Mine Run Campaign. During the battle, Dr. Hezlop carried at least one wounded man off the field on his back before taking charge of the hospital and assisting in the treatment of the wounded men as they came in. According to Dr. William Reznor, the surgeon of the Sixth Ohio Cavalry, the custom was to do "simple dressings of the wounded brought into the hospital during the time of the engagement" and not to do the more complicated operations until "after the engagement ceases." Dr. Reznor also testified that there was only one operation performed by Dr. Hezlep that day. Although the operation was "well completed and terminated well," Dr. Hezlep made a "mis-cut" during the amputation of the patient's arm. Dr. Reznor attributed Dr. Hezlep's mistake to "excitement" and testified that, although he had seen Dr. Hezlep drinking during the day and thought that he may have been "slightly under the influence earlier in the afternoon," he was not intoxicated at the time the surgery was done.

The surgeon for the Fourth Pennsylvania Cavalry, who was also at the battle, testified that he had seen Dr. Hezlep drinking whiskey during the day and that it had

A Union doctor prepares for an amputation. (National Archives)

"a considerable effect on him," but that by the time he performed the amputation he was no longer intoxicated. Another witness, assistant surgeon Isaiah Everhart, who had assisted Dr. Hezlep, "judged him to be slightly under the influence of alcohol, but not sufficient to unfit him from performing his duties." Lieutenant Colonel Edward Jones, the only line officer who testified at the trial, appeared as a witness for the defense. "During the time I was there, Dr. Hezlep did not appear intoxicated.... I consider [him to be] an excitable man, but not a drinking man." As no witness came forward with testimony more damning than the fact that Dr. Hezlep had "talked loudly" and had made movements that were "rapid and unnatural," the court found him not guilty. Dr. Hezlep may have been drinking, but according to the court he was not too drunk to perform his duty. Dr. Hezlep went on to serve as a surgeon in the army for the rest of the war.

Strange but True Doctor Stories

According to Union Surgeon General William Hammond, "the Civil War was fought at the end of the medical Middle Ages." The doctors who volunteered to serve during the Civil War were part of the last generation of physicians to treat patients without the benefit of the advances made by Louis Pasteur, who discovered microscopic organisms, and Joseph Lister, who proved the benefits of antiseptics during surgery. As a result, the odds of a soldier dying from disease were roughly 10 times higher during the Civil War than they were in World War I. In fact, more than 45,000 Union soldiers died as a result of diarrhea and dysentery, and another 46,000 succumbed to the fevers of typhoid and malaria. In addition, a wounded Civil War soldier was eight times more likely to die as a result of his wounds than was a World War I soldier.

To become a doctor in 1861, a medical student had to attend 18 months of lectures at a medical school. Because the schools were in business to make money, very few prospective students were turned away and even fewer flunked out. In addition, there were no official medical standards or regulatory bodies to ensure a minimum level of competency for either the medical school or its graduates. If you could afford the tuition and attended the lectures, you became a doctor. The different fields available to a doctor in 1861 included homeopathy, naturopathy, hydropathy, and allopathy. Most conventional doctors fell into the allopathy category, which divided all diseases into two categories: *sthenic* diseases, which involved a rapid pulse, fever, and an agitated condition, and *asthenic* diseases, which resulted in low pulses and decreased energy. Stenthic patients were treated with laxatives and emetics, to drain away excess "tissue excitement," while asthenic patients were given alcohol and other tonics to "stimulate" their weakened condition.

Despite the lack of recognized standards, the Union army struggled to make sure its doctors were adequately trained and reasonably knowledgeable. Early in the war, regimental commanders usually appointed a surgeon for their unit, but this proved to be a less than ideal solution and these surgeons probably did as much harm as they did good. Eventually, all surgeons who wanted a commission in the medical corps were required to pass a rigorous five-hour oral examination. When the Sanitary Commission inspected the medical facilities of the Union army, only two percent of the doctors were found to be incompetent. This two percent however, usually escaped notice until they did something so outrageous that even the Union army had to take note.

Sketch, by Arthur Lumley, of wounded soldiers being transported to a field hospital. (Library of Congress)

Charles E. Briggs: Doctor or Veterinarian

A graduate of Harvard Medical School in 1856, Dr. Briggs was a veteran of a year's service as an assistant surgeon before transferring to the 54th Massachusetts Colored Infantry in the fall of 1863. The 54th Massachusetts had been recruited from free African-American men from that state and had made a name for itself during its unsuccessful assault on Battery Wagner on July 18, 1863. The assault (recreated in the movie *Glory*) cost the Massachusetts unit more than 25 percent of its men, but in light of the way they continued to press the attack on a well-entrenched Confederate position and the fact that they almost won, despite their fearful casualties, the action was seen by many as proof that black men could fight well in battle. Since that time, the 54th Massachusetts had not seen any major action while garrisoning Morris Island as part of the siege of Charleston.

Dr. Briggs's tenure with the 54th Massachusetts was uneventful until the night of November 6, 1863, when he was called to the stables to examine Private James Riley. It seems Riley was suspected of having a "sexual connexion with a mare." Briggs examined Riley's clothes, as well as the horse, and despite a few questionable findings, testified, "My examination did not conclusively prove Riley had intercourse with the mare." Based on Briggs's testimony, Private Riley was found not guilty. But, the story did not end there.

After the trial, Dr. Briggs had Private Riley brought to his tent and placed two guards outside. Feeling justified in his actions against a black man, Briggs then ordered Riley "stripped, gagged, and bound down upon a bed," where Briggs performed a circumcision upon him—without using anesthesia. To make the surgery even more painful, Briggs used a hot iron to cauterize the incision. For his actions, Dr. Briggs was charged with inflicting the "act of circumcision as a punishment" and neglecting to "take measures to alleviate the pain." Incredibly, Dr. Briggs never faced a court-martial for his actions. Instead, he was promoted to full surgeon of the 54th Massachusetts a few weeks later and served with the unit until it was mustered out at the end of the war.

George H. Mitchell: Three-Time Loser

Dr. George Mitchell had the dubious honor of being court-martialed three times while serving as an assistant surgeon in the Union army. The first court-martial occurred after Dr. Mitchell was involved in a fist fight with the regimental quartermaster. There is no record of what the fight was about, but Dr. Mitchell and Lieutenant Fritz were observed fighting by the regimental commander Colonel McClean. The colonel ordered both men to their quarters, but they continued fighting until they were both put under arrest. Dr. Mitchell admitted using "harsh words" to Lieutenant Fritz, but testified that he could not obey the colonel's order to stop fighting because his arms were "so enveloped in an India Rubber Coat" that he was "utterly unable to obey the order of the colonel." The court did not accept Dr. Mitchell's defense, and he was found guilty and ordered dismissed from the service.

While Dr. Mitchell's appeal was pending, he was again court-martialed, this time for appropriating "twenty pounds of beef, two cans of condensed milk, three cans of preserved fruit, and one package of Oswego starch." The charges stemmed from Dr. Mitchell's behavior while his unit was on the march near Keedysville, Maryland, shortly after the battle of Antietam. According to an ambulance driver for the 88th Pennsylvania Infantry, Dr. Mitchell took "two cans of condensed milk, one can of beef tea and some liquor," and that the next day he requisitioned 25 pounds of beef from a supply depot, which was supposed to be delivered to the hospital. Due to the extreme confusion following the battle, Dr. Mitchell was acquitted of the charges, but the reviewing general admonished Mitchell for his behavior.

In June 1863, Dr. Mitchell's appeal of his first court-martial was officially denied by President Lincoln. However, a copy of the order was never received at regimental headquarters and he continued to serve as an assistant surgeon. Despite the two court-martials on his record, Dr. Mitchell was promoted to major and full surgeon of the regiment on August 15, 1863. He was court-martialed a third time in December 1864, this time for "fraudulently appropriating U.S. government lumber," which he had delivered to his own house along with "fifteen pounds of ten-penny nails, one barrel of lime, a bucket, and a broom." Dr. Mitchell, who was attached to the Haddington Army Hospital in Philadelphia, Pennsylvania, at the time, also arranged for "the chief carpenter, the mason, laborers, and various patients and employees" at the hospital to work on his home in the city. To make matters worse, Dr. Mitchell was also charged with being $40 short on his accounting of the hospital fund. This time, Dr. Mitchell could not get away with his transgressions. He was found guilty and, once again, dismissed from the service with the added caveat that he "be forever disqualified from holding any position of honor or profit in the military service of the United States."

Edward Flynn: The Sting

Dr. Edward Flynn was a contract physician at the Benton Barracks in St. Louis, Missouri. As a contract physician, Dr. Flynn served as an acting assistant surgeon, but held no commission in the army. During the war, approximately 5,000 contract physicians were hired to work in overcrowded hospitals in the North. In addition to his duties as a contract physician, Dr. Flynn also served on the medical examining board for sick and wounded soldiers being considered for discharge from the army. When the assistant surgeon general Robert Wood received an anonymous letter that some of the doctors at Benton Barracks were accepting money for fraudulent discharges, he decided to run a sting operation. Acting at Wood's behest, Ira Russell, the surgeon-in-chief at Benton Barracks, enlisted the aid of Private Benjamin Wilkins. Wilkins, who had been captured at Holly Springs, Mississippi, was considered a paroled prisoner and could not return to his unit until he had been properly exchanged. In the interim, Private Wilkins worked as an aide at the Benton Barracks hospital. Wilkins was instructed by Dr. Russell to ask Dr. Flynn for a discharge in exchange for $50. According to Wilkins's testimony, Dr. Flynn made a slight objection, but finally agreed to the proposition. Wilkins also testified that Dr. Flynn told him, "I don't blame any soldier for getting his discharge when he can."

When it came time for the physical examination of Wilkins, Dr. Flynn spent about five minutes before determining that Wilkins had valvular heart disease and was unfit for further military service. Dr. Flynn then took the money that Wilkins had offered him. At the hearing, Private Wilkins was examined by two other doctors to determine whether he really suffered from valvular heart disease. Dr. William Grier diagnosed Private Wilkins with slight hypertrophy but not heart valve disease. Dr. James Hall, who also served on the medical examining board, testified that Wilkins suffered from bilious fever and torpidity of the liver, but that these conditions did not warrant a discharge from the service. After considering the testimony, Dr. Flynn was found guilty and dismissed from the service. In addition, Flynn was ordered to forfeit all pay due to him and was sentenced to 60 days in the Myrtle Street Military Prison. Dr. Flynn had his prison sentence commuted by the reviewing officer on September 15, 1863, but his dismissal remained in force. He applied for a military pension 18 years later, but was denied, due to his poor service record.

CHAPTER 11

SICK AND WOUNDED GENERALS IN THE CONFEDERATE ARMY

Thomas Fenton Toon: North Carolina's Finest

The state of North Carolina contributed more than 125,000 soldiers, or about one-sixth of the men in the Confederate army. In fact, for most of the last two years of the war, half of Robert E. Lee's Army of Northern Virginia was made up of North Carolina regiments. By the time the war ended, 63,000 North Carolinian men had died on the battlefield or from disease. North Carolina also contributed the most wounded general in the Confederate army. Little known Thomas Toon from Columbus County, North Carolina, was the only Confederate general to be wounded in seven different engagements. Surprisingly, Toon survived the war and didn't die until 1902 of heart failure. Toon was a student at Wake Forrest when the war started. He enlisted, along with his brother William, in the 20th North Carolina Infantry and was elected lieutenant in 1861. He was wounded for the first time at the battle of Seven Pines on May 31, 1862 by a musket ball that had passed through another man. He was wounded again during the Seven Days' Battle, but recovered to rejoin his unit in July 1862. The following winter, Toon—along with many other officers in the 20th North Carolina—rebelled when their brigade commander, General Alfred Iverson, tried to appoint a friend of his as colonel of the regiment. Tensions between Iverson and the regimental officers escalated when Iverson tried to arrest all 26 officers for writing a letter of protest to the inspector general of the army. Eventually, a compromise was reached, and Toon was selected for promotion to the position of colonel of the regiment.

At the battle of Chancellorsville—his first battle as regimental commander of the 20th North Carolina—Toon was wounded three times. The first wound occurred early in the morning, but Toon remained on the field to lead his men during General Stonewall Jackson's flank attack. Late in the day, Toon was hit twice more and forced to leave the field. He recovered in time to lead the 20th North Carolina at Gettysburg, where General Iverson marched them into Forney's Field "as evenly as if on parade." Unfortunately, the incompetent Iverson, who was hiding in the rear, neglected to send out any skirmishers, and Toon's men were surprised by Union soldiers who popped up from behind a stone wall and started firing, with devastating results. Later in the day, a Virginia artillerist counted, within "a few feet," 79 North Carolina soldiers "lying dead in a straight line." Despite the gruesome casualty rate that nearly obliterated his unit, Toon escaped injury. (After the Forney's Field debacle, Iverson was removed from the army.) Toon was not wounded again until the battle of Spotsylvania, where he was hit in the leg by a spent bullet. After only a few days, he had recovered sufficiently to accept a promotion to brigadier general. Toon commanded a brigade during General Early's advance on Washington and at the battle of Monocacy. In August 1864, Toon gave up his promotion (rather than leave the unit) when General Robert Johnston recovered from his injuries and returned to command. He was wounded for the seventh and last time at Hare's Hill, just weeks before the war came to an end. While rallying his men, General Toon was hit when he stood on top of the breastworks during Lee's last attack of the war, on Fort Steadman. Toon was taken back to his home in North Carolina where he fully recovered and embarked on a postwar career as a banker.

Union Fort Steadman, scene of General Lee's last major attack of the war and of General Toon's seventh and last wound. (Library of Congress)

Daniel Adams: Left for Dead

Daniel Adams, a native of Frankfort, Kentucky, was practicing law in Louisiana when the Civil War began. No stranger to violence (he had shot and killed a newspaper editor in a duel in 1843), Adams quickly accepted a commission with the First Louisiana Regulars as a lieutenant colonel. (Adams's brother, William Wirt Adams, also joined the Confederate army and was promoted to brigadier general in 1863.) Early in the morning on the first day of the battle of Shiloh, General Adley Gladden was mortally wounded when he was struck by a cannonball, and Adams took over as commander of the First Louisiana. Later that same day, in fighting around the Hornet's Nest, Adams was struck in the head by a musket ball. The bullet struck Adams above the left eye and exited his skull behind his left ear.

Helpless and insensible, Adams was taken to a field hospital and later thrown into a wagon that was transporting wounded men back to Corinth, Mississippi. The driver of the wagon, seeing no signs of life, threw Adams's body along the road to help lighten his load

General Adams was shot in the head while attacking the Union stronghold called the Hornet's Nest, during the battle of Shiloh. (Library of Congress)

as he tried to negotiate his way along the muddy route. Left for dead in the mud, Adams was saved when men from the Tenth Mississippi noticed signs of life and hurried him to a nearby hospital. Incredibly, Adams survived his injuries and was promoted to brigadier general on May 23, 1862.

Four months after his wounding at Shiloh, General Adams was pronounced fit for duty. Now commanding the Louisiana Brigade, Adams participated in the battles at Perryville and Murfreesboro, where his left arm was wounded by a shell fragment. Adams again recovered from his wounds, rejoined the army in September, and participated in the battle of Chickamauga. There he was wounded for a third time and left on the battlefield to be captured. He was taken to a Union hospital where the musket ball, which was embedded in his arm, was removed, along with two inches of bone. After four weeks, Adams again recovered from his injuries. He was paroled and returned to the Confederate lines, where he served the remainder of the war as commander of the

District of Central Alabama. When the war ended, he returned to his law practice in New Orleans, Louisiana, until his death in 1872.

Nathan Bedford Forrest: Riding With the Devil

The general with the strongest powers of recuperation had to be Nathan Bedford Forrest. Forrest was shot for the first time in 1845 when he was involved in a street fight in Hernando, Mississippi. Forrest's first wound during the Civil War occurred on February 15, 1862, when a cannonball passed just behind his legs and through his horse. The day after the battle of Shiloh, Forrest was wounded in a cavalry charge, during which he picked up a small Union soldier and used him as a shield. A musket ball entered just above Forrest's left hip, went through his back muscles, and lodged against his spinal column. The wound was considered mortal, but Forrest survived and the ball was removed without anesthetic three weeks later. After being confined to his bed for only two weeks, Forrest was back in the saddle. One of the many injuries Forrest received in falls from his horse occurred in September 1862, when he was thrown from the animal and dislocated his right shoulder. As usual, he recovered quickly.

General Forrest's second "mortal" wound occurred on June 13, 1863, when he was confronted by Lieutenant Andrew Wills Gould. The 23-year-old artillerist was angered by a transfer Forrest had ordered after Gould had lost two artillery pieces. Believing that Gould was going to attack him, Forrest pulled out a pocketknife. Gould responded by shooting Forrest in the stomach with a large caliber pistol. Forrest then killed Gould by stabbing him. When Forrest was examined by a doctor, it was found that the bullet had penetrated his body without striking any vital organs. Although he lost a lot of blood, Forrest was again back in the saddle in less than two weeks, without having the bullet removed from his body.

General Forrest was wounded for the third time on July 15, 1864, during the battle of Tupelo. This time, he was shot in the big toe on his right foot. Despite his previous grievous injuries, this wound proved to be the most painful of them all.

Statue of Nathan Bedford Forrest, located in Forrest Park in Memphis, Tennessee. (Library of Congress)

Forrest was incapacitated for more than a month and forced to ride in a farm buggy. His final combat wound occurred in April 1865, when Forrest received saber wounds to his head, shoulders, and arms, in a battle at Ebenezer Church, Alabama. Forrest shook off these wounds and was back in the saddle the next day. After the war, Forrest returned to his plantation, where he faced a medical condition that he could not defeat—diabetes. Weakened by chronic diarrhea, Forrest became so frail by the summer of 1877 that he couldn't get up without help. A shadow of his former self, Forrest weighed little more than a hundred pounds at the time of his death a few weeks later.

Dick Ewell and Francis Nicholls:
Losing an Arm and a Leg

During the Civil War, 24 Confederate generals suffered through the amputation of a limb. (Eight other generals received wounds that warranted amputation, but refused the operation.) Of the 18 generals who had a leg amputated, only seven survived the operation. General Richard Ewell was the most senior general to lose a leg. A veteran of the Mexican and Indian Wars, Ewell had had his share of physical maladies before the Civil War. In 1841, he got the nickname "Old Bald Head," when he contracted malaria and cut off all his hair because it was falling out. To recover, he ate only raw tomatoes, onions, salt, sweet potatoes, and dried beef. When the war started, Ewell suffered from vertigo, nausea, and dyspepsia. To combat these problems, Ewell again made use of a special diet that included very little except frumenty (made of hulled wheat boiled in milk and sugar). In May 1862, after he had been promoted to major general, Ewell complained of severe headaches and the worst dyspepsia he had ever experienced. ("Dyspepsia" was a catch-all diagnosis that involved everything in the stomach and gastric system.)

General Ewell was leading a division in Stonewall Jackson's corps during the battle at Second Manassas when he was wounded near the small town of Groveton, Virginia, by a minié ball that hit the center of his kneecap. Ewell wasn't found until after dark. Alive but in great pain, he was taken from the

Despite losing a leg, General Richard Ewell commanded a corps in the Army of Northern Virginia. (Library of Congress)

field. At first doctors thought they could save the leg, but when Dr. Hunter McGuire examined Ewell the next morning, he discovered that the patella had been split in two and the head of the tibia had splintered. Dr. McGuire operated that afternoon and didn't expect Ewell to survive the operation. When the operation was concluded, Ewell was given brandy every 15 minutes to dull the pain. To aid his recovery, Ewell adopted a diet of grapes, fruit, and Madeira wine. In many ways,

Ewell's recovery was even more painful than the initial surgery. On Christmas Day 1862, he slipped on some ice and reopened the wound, knocking off another inch of bone. The following spring, when he finally recovered enough to move around again, he forgot about his missing leg and tried to walk. Once again the wound reopened, and Ewell lost a great deal of blood.

Despite his infirmities, General Lee promoted Ewell to lieutenant general and gave him command of a corps in the Army of Northern Virginia. After he got the news on May 23, 1863, the 46-year-old Ewell took the time to get married to his cousin Lizinka Campbell Brown. Ewell rejoined the army six days later, after an absence of nine months, to take command of the Second Corps of Lee's army at the beginning of the Gettysburg campaign. Initially, Ewell did very well in his new position. He won a battle in Winchester, Virginia, and his corps led the army into Pennsylvania. However, on the eve of the battle of Gettysburg, Ewell was thoroughly worn out from the campaigning. Sapped of his strength, Ewell performed poorly during the battle, often deferring to his subordinate General Jubal Early. During the next winter, Ewell contracted osteomyelitis (an infectious inflammatory disease of the bone) and had to be hospitalized. He recovered sufficiently to resume command, but had to travel in an ambulance. By June 1864, Ewell's condition had deteriorated to the point where General Lee felt obligated to reassign him to the less strenuous position as commander of the Petersburg defenses. During the siege of Petersburg, Ewell fell from his horse and reopened his old wound. He remained with his men and was captured during the battle of Saylor's Creek, on April 6, 1865. While a prisoner, Ewell began suffering from neuralgia, a condition that lasted through the rest of his life. After the war, Ewell retired to his farm near Spring Hill, Tennessee, and was one of the very few Civil War generals who did not feel compelled to write about his experiences. Ewell's various illnesses and wounds took their toll, and he died at the relatively young age of 55 after contracting typhoid pneumonia.

The only Confederate general to suffer the amputation of an arm *and* a leg was Francis Nicholls. The Louisiana native was almost denied admission to West Point because of varicose veins and suffered from very poor health while serving in Florida and California before the Civil War. In 1856, he was forced to retire from the army, due to chronic gastric problems and embarked on a less strenuous career as a lawyer. He joined the Confederate army in 1861, as captain of the Phoenix Guards, but was soon elected to colonel of the Eighth Louisiana Volunteers. Nicholls led the regiment at First Manassas and during Stonewall Jackson's Shenandoah Valley Campaign in the spring of 1862. Nicholls was wounded for the first time when a minié ball hit his left elbow during fighting outside Winchester, Virginia, on May 25, 1862. He was taken to a hospital in Winchester where doctors tried to save the arm, but were eventually forced to amputate. Nicholls was given only whiskey to dull the pain, but the operation was a success and he was promoted to brigadier general. After recuperating for almost a year, Nicholls returned to duty in March of 1863.

At the battle of Chancellorsville, Nicholls was wounded in the left foot by a shell fragment during nighttime fighting. Unable to see, Nicholls reached for his boot and discovered that it and his foot were gone. Expecting to bleed to death, Nicholls was found by his men, who carried him on a blanket, under heavy fire, to the rear. Rather than waste time transporting him to a hospital, Nicholls's leg was amputated in a small tent. He was taken to Lynchburg, Virginia, where he was taken care of in a private home. He eventually recovered from his wounds and was appointed commander of the small Confederate force in Lynchburg in August 1863. A year later, when Lynchburg was threatened by Union forces commanded by General David Hunter, the one-armed, one-egged Nicholls rode out to his men to inform them that additional troops were on the way. By the time Hunter advanced, the reinforcements had reached the city to help repulse the attack. Nicholls served out the rest of the war as commander of the Bureau of Conscription in the Trans-Mississippi Department. After the war, Nicholls served two terms as governor of Louisiana and as a justice on the Louisiana Supreme Court. He finally died, in 1911, after contracting pneumonia.

Lee, Beauregard, and Bragg: The Strain of Command

Every general officer who commanded an army during the Civil War suffered from the stress and fatigue inherent in the position. When General Robert E. Lee returned from western Virginia after his first combat command, his hair and beard had turned gray. By the time he led his army to Gettysburg two years later, Lee suffered from chest and back pains, high blood pressure, chronic diarrhea, and rheumatism. In October 1863, the rheumatism had become so bad that he could not mount a horse by himself. The pain grew stronger in December and he seemed to age overnight when his hair and beard turned white. Unable to rest and recuperate during the spring and summer of 1864 due to General Grant's incessant attacks, Lee was forced to retire to his tent for two days during the battle of North Anna. This was extremely unfortunate as Lee had maneuvered Grant's army into a precarious position where its two wings were separated by the North Anna River. Grant soon realized his predicament and withdrew his army back across the river. Unwilling to trust the attack to a subordinate commander, Lee's best opportunity to stop Grant's advance towards Richmond was lost as he lay incapacitated in his headquarters tent.

General Lee's condition gradually got better, but he still suffered from bouts of sciatica, lumbago, and rheumatism for the rest of the war. After the war, Lee accepted a position as president of Washington College in Lexington, Virginia. Still suffering the effects of his wartime service, Lee regularly took the waters at White Sulpher Springs. His health continued to deteriorate, and by the summer of 1868, Lee could no longer ride his horse. He was confined to his bed early in 1870, and in September, he lost the ability to speak. In an effort to treat Lee, doctors gave him hot foot baths and cold compresses, blisters were applied behind his ears, he was given a purgative enema, and six ounces of blood were drawn. Lee seemed to improve in the early part of October but soon suffered a relapse and died on October 12, 1870. Modern doctors attribute Lee's final illness to a stroke, but at the time, it was thought that Lee had died because his heart strings had been broken at Appomattox.

General Robert E. Lee was too sick to launch an attack against isolated Union forces sent across the North Anna River in May 1864. (Library of Congress)

General Pierre Gustave Toutant Beauregard's fall from grace in June 1862, after he left the army due to illness, was as sudden and surprising as was his rapid assent after Fort Sumter. Before the war, Beauregard had served as superintendent of West Point, but he resigned his commission to become a brigadier general in the Confederate army. Assigned to Charleston, South Carolina, Beauregard followed President Davis's instructions and opened fire on Fort Sumter on April 12, 1861. Hailed as the "Hero of Sumter," Beauregard was given command of the main Confederate army in Virginia and received much of the acclaim for the victory at First Manassas. However, the colorful Creole suffered from a chronic throat ailment that had bothered him since he was a boy. The problem with his throat reappeared shortly after the battle at First Manassas, and Beauregard had throat surgery in January 1862. He ignored the advice of his physicians, who wanted him to rest, and traveled to Tennessee a month later to resume his military duties. He assumed command of the army at Shiloh, when General A.S. Johnston was mortally wounded, and supervised the subsequent retreat to Corinth, Mississippi. Finally, in June 1862, Beauregard heeded the advice of his physicians who wanted him to rest and seek treatment at Bladon's Springs. It was six months before Beauregard was well enough to resume his duties, but by then his hopes of commanding a major army in the field were gone. Still bothered by throat problems, he was assigned to the Department of South Carolina and Georgia, because his health was considered too fragile to withstand the cold weather. Beauregard was again forced to seek treatment in April 1864, but returned to duty shortly after, "willing to serve the cause to the utter sacrifice of his health." During the periods he was healthy enough to command, Beauregard performed well. He fought off several Union attempts to take Charleston and saved General Lee's army with his stout defense of Petersburg, Virginia, in May 1864. After the war, Beauregard thrived as a railroad president, a lottery official, and as adjutant general for his home state of Louisiana. He died at the age of 75, as a result of heart disease.

General Braxton Bragg was another general who's precarious health suffered when he was elevated to commander of an army. Before the war, Bragg had a very thin "cadaverous appearance" and suffered from intermittent migraine headaches, dyspepsia, and chronic dysentery. A West Point graduate and veteran of war in Florida and Mexico, Bragg resigned due to health problems in 1856. He returned to military life, joining the Confederate army as a brigadier general in March 1861. Quickly promoted to major general, Bragg took command of the Army of Mississippi in June 1862 when Beauregard sought medical treatment. By the spring of 1863, his staff was so concerned about his health and his failure to eat properly that they began serving him meals while he was working at his desk. In May 1863, while with the army in Middle Tennessee, Bragg had an outbreak of painful boils and chronic diarrhea, which hampered his ability to counter Union General William Rosecrans's skillful Tullahoma Campaign. The defeat cost the Confederacy control over both Chattanooga and Knoxville, Tennessee. By this time, Bragg was in such poor health that he could barely continue his duties, and in August 1863 he was forced to leave the army to seek treatment at a hospital in Cherokee Springs, Georgia. He recovered sufficiently to rejoin the army and win his only significant battlefield victory at Chickamauga in September. However, Bragg allowed Rosecrans's army to escape to Chattanooga when he did not follow up on his victory. After the battle, Bragg's headquarters was in such a turmoil that President Jefferson Davis felt compelled to visit the army and restore order. While it was clear to all of his subordinate commanders that Bragg was no longer physically or mentally fit to command an army in the field, Davis allowed Bragg to remain. When he suffered another defeat a month later at the hands of General Grant, Bragg was finally relieved of command. He went to Warm Springs, Georgia, to recuperate, and once his health was restored, he served as a military advisor to President Davis for the duration of the war. Bragg worked as an engineer after the war in Alabama and Texas until his sudden death (probably due to a heart attack) at the age of 59.

Garnett, Hunton, and Kemper:
The Horsemen of Pickett's Charge

On the afternoon of July 3, 1863, 15,000 Confederate soldiers started marching across a half mile of open field towards the Union lines at Gettysburg, in what has come to be known as Pickett's Charge. General Richard Garnett commanded one of the 10 brigades that participated in the charge, and he was one of only three men to make the charge on horseback. The 46-year-old general, whose older brother

General Richard Garnett was killed on horseback, while leading his men, during Pickett's Charge. (Library of Congress)

Robert was the first Confederate general to die during the Civil War, had served bravely in the military for his entire adult life. However, Garnett's military record was stained when he was arrested by General Stonewall Jackson for withdrawing his brigade without orders, during the battle of Kernstown, in April 1862. By all accounts, Garnett's actions were entirely reasonable, as his men were greatly outnumbered and running low on ammunition. However, Jackson did not see it that way and had Garnett arrested and charged with neglect of duty. The case languished for months due to the lack of available senior officers for a court-martial. Garnett was eventually brought to trial on August 6, 1862, but he was released when General Jackson was ordered away and the case was eventually dropped after Jackson was killed. Seeking to restore his honor, Garnett was unwilling to exempt himself from the infantry charge, even though he had been kicked in the ankle a month before Gettysburg and could not walk. He led his brigade on horseback and was practically cut in half by grapeshot during Pickett's Charge. His body was never identified after the battle, and he was probably buried on the field, in an unmarked grave.

The other two generals who rode horses during Pickett's Charge were James Kemper and Eppa Hunton. Kemper, another of Pickett's brigade commanders, was too sick to lead the charge on foot. A member of the Virginia Delegates, Kemper was seriously wounded by a minié ball, which hit him on the inside of his left thigh. The ball ricocheted off Kemper's femur and lodged near the base of his spine, leaving him paralyzed. Kemper was captured during the retreat from Gettysburg and sent to a hospital in Baltimore to recuperate. General Eppa Hunton suffered from the effects of an anal fistula throughout his service in the Confederate army. Although Hunton had surgery to correct the condition in November 1861, he had twice been judged to be unfit for command before being allowed to rejoin the regiment prior to Gettysburg. Still too sick to walk across the field, Hunton rode his horse during Pickett's Charge and was wounded in the right leg, just below the knee. Because his horse had also been shot, Hunton struggled to the rear, on foot, where an ambulance carried him back to a field hospital. Hunton recovered and returned to the military, despite his ongoing problems with the fistula. It wasn't until after he was captured at Saylor's Creek, in April 1865, and brought to Fort Warren that a change of diet helped Hunton regain his strength.

Joe Johnston: Honorable Mention

General Joseph Johnston endured a tumultuous career as one of the most controversial generals in the Confederate army. A national hero after the great victory at Manassas, Johnston's descent began when he was wounded, in May 1862, and lost command of the largest Confederate field army to Robert E. Lee. However, this was not the first time Joe Johnston had been wounded in battle. In fact, the wounding at Seven Pines followed a pattern in which Johnston was severely injured in (almost) every engagement he took part in. The first time he was wounded was in 1838, while fighting in Florida during the Seminole War. Ambushed at Jupiter Inlet, Florida, Johnston was hit in the forehead by a bullet, which passed around his skull. Although Johnston thought he was mortally wounded, when he realized no bones had been broken he got up and continued to fight.

General Joe Johnston was severely wounded on the Seven Pines battlefield. (Library of Congress)

He was wounded for a second time, in 1847, during the Mexican War, at the battle at Cerro Gordo. This time he was struck twice by musket fire. He recovered in time to take part in the battle of Chapultepec five months later, where he was also wounded. Johnston managed to avoid being injured in battle for the first time when he emerged unscathed after Manassas. However, his luck ran out at Seven Pines, when he was struck in the right shoulder by a musket and hit in the chest by a shell fragment. When examined by a surgeon, Johnston was found to have broken two ribs and his shoulder blade. The treatment prescribed was "bleeding, blistering, depletion of the system." It took Johnston a full year to recover from his injuries and return to the army. After Seven Pines, Johnston was able to avoid any further battlefield injuries, but he was never able to reclaim his role as the most important general in the Confederate army. He enjoyed good health in later life until he attended General William T. Sherman's funeral in 1891. While there, the 84-year-old Johnston supposedly refused to wear a hat and contracted a deadly cold. However, Johnston's death certificate stated that he died of heart failure.

PART FIVE

THE AFTERMATH

Much of what we know—or think we know about the Civil War—resulted from the efforts of men who sought to put their imprint on the war. One such man was John Bachelder who, more than anyone else, was responsible for the public face of the Gettysburg battlefield. While some may still believe Winston Churchill was correct when he said that only victors write history, it is more accurate to say that those who care the most and work the hardest are those who dominate how history is written and remembered. This is evident in how the great fire in Columbia, South Carolina, has been portrayed. Despite an avalanche of contrary evidence, the idea that General William T. Sherman wantonly burned Southern cities has crept into our modern consciousness. One example is a reference made, in Richard Clark's recent best-selling work *Against All Enemies*, to imaginary orders from Washington to burn Atlanta "to the ground." These and other continuing controversies will be examined in this section of the book, to see how they compare with some of the popular conceptions held about the war.

CHAPTER 12

THE MONUMENTAL BATTLE OF GETTYSBURG

Bachelder's Battlefield

John Bachelder was a landscape painter from Maine who was trying to gather enough material to make an historically accurate painting of the battle of Bunker Hill, when the Civil War erupted in 1861. Rather than continue with his increasingly frustrating endeavor, Bachelder decided upon a new course of action. He would seek out the "decisive battle" of the Civil War, learn its details, and eventually prepare the authoritative account of the battle. Throughout 1862 Bachelder traveled with the Army of the Potomac seeking the decisive battle, until illness eventually forced him to return home. However, within days of the battle of Gettysburg, Bachelder returned to the army. Convinced that this was the decisive battle he had been seeking, he began interviewing as many wounded soldiers as he could find. He even received permission from General Meade to remain with the army and spent the entire winter of 1863 interviewing hundreds of soldiers who had fought at Gettysburg.

After the war ended, Bachelder continued gathering information about the battle until he had visited every regiment and battery in the Army of the Potomac and interviewed 26 different generals involved in the battle. Although Bachelder was convinced that Gettysburg was the decisive battle that defined the course of the Civil War, it wasn't until 1869 that he stumbled upon an idea that would cement his vision of the battle in the minds of the general public. Bachelder focused his attention on Pickett's Charge and identified a small grove of trees located near the center of the battlefield behind a small stone wall as the exact spot where the war was decided. Bachelder named the spot the "Copse of Trees." The Union defensive position along the stone wall became "The Angle," and the entire area was christened the "High Water Mark of the Confederacy." To make this more evident to visitors of the battlefield, Bachelder surrounded the trees with an iron fence and raised money for a prominent monument to permanently mark the spot. To further his vision of the battlefield, Bachelder commissioned a well-known artist to create a painting that depicted the climactic scene, and he then sold thousands of lithographs of the image.

In 1880 Bachelder's reputation as the nation's leading authority on Gettysburg was solidified when the United States Congress awarded him with a $50,000 grant—a sum equal to a senator's pay for 10 years—to write the official history of the battle. Bachelder was also appointed as superintendent of the Gettysburg Battlefield Memorial Association. This position gave him full authority for the placement and wording on all monuments erected on the battlefield. Bachelder's authority over the battlefield eventually became so complete that even Union generals who were in the battle yielded to his opinion of what happened. When General Hancock, the commander of the Union troops who defended The Angle, marked the spot where he had been wounded, Bachelder moved it to a place more in keeping with his version of the events. All Hancock could do was request that a "stake or small boulder" be placed on the spot he had identified.

The supreme irony of Bachelder's endeavor is that, despite his years of dedication and research, he never finished his official history of the battle. He did publish a 2,000-page summary of the battle, but that was supplanted by the publication of the *Official Records* by the War Department. However, Bachelder's vision of the battlefield did become a permanent fixture in the public consciousness, and the sites that are his legacy—the Copse of Trees, The Angle, and the High Water Mark—remain the best marked and most visited places on the battlefield. This, despite that "there is no credible evidence that anyone pointed to the angle in the stone fence or the copse of trees" before the assault or that Lee could have won the war by winning the battle. The widely held belief that Gettysburg was the turning point of the war is much more a product of Bachelder's marketing efforts than the research done by the legions of historians who have studied the battle.

John Bachelder's High Water Mark monument at Gettysburg battlefield. (Library of Congress)

The Copse of Trees:
Monumental Battles at The Angle

John Bachelder's successful effort to establish the ground where Pickett's Charge crashed against The Angle as the most important part of the most important battlefield of the Civil War spurred the desire of Union units, who defended that portion of the field, to build monuments along the stone wall. On July 3, 1887, veterans from the 69th and 71st Pennsylvania Infantry each dedicated monuments along The Angle. However, veterans from the 72nd Pennsylvania ran into a storm of protest when they also tried to place a monument near the stone wall.

During the battle the 72nd Pennsylvania had been held in reserve in case of a Confederate breakthrough. The problem was that, when the Confederates did threaten to break the line, the men of 72nd Pennsylvania refused to advance. However, they still wanted their monument in a place of honor near the stone wall. When the Gettysburg Battlefield Memorial Association refused to allow this, the men of the 72nd Pennsylvania filed a lawsuit. To hedge their bet they also purchased a small plot of land on the other side of the stone wall for their monument, in case their legal efforts failed. However, the Pennsylvania Supreme Court eventually ruled in their favor, and on July 4, 1891, the survivors of the 72nd Pennsylvania Infantry dedicated their very own monument near The Angle. A year later, when a monument for the 42nd New York Infantry was being dedicated, *behind* the 72nd Pennsylvania monument, General Dan Sickles had this to say: "I cannot perform this duty without giving expression to the…indignation felt by the veterans of this famous battalion when they see their monument standing in a rear line…, whilst troops that refused to advance…are permitted to place their monument on a line much further to the front than they ventured to march, until after the victory was won."

The Confederate veterans of Pickett's Division also wanted to place a monument along The Angle to commemorate the High Water Mark of their charge. However, the Gettysburg Battlefield Memorial Association denied them permission and they eventually placed their monument near General Pickett's grave in the Hollywood Cemetery in Richmond, Virginia. In 1884, they did allow a marker to be placed on the spot where General Armistead was killed while leading the charge. While the marker itself did not cause any controversy, its placement did, as both sides had a vested interest in putting the marker much further inside The Angle than any contemporary account of Armistead's death had placed him. The reason for this was simple: the further that Armistead got, the closer the Confederates came to ultimate victory and the more valiant were the Union defenders who denied him the victory. Today, instead of the four or five feet that Armistead made it past the stone wall before his death, the marker identifying the spot is almost 85 feet past the wall.

The state of North Carolina had to wait another hundred years to honor the High Water Mark of the units from that state at Gettysburg. While Pickett's Charge is remembered as mainly a Virginian affair, half the men that took part in the charge were from North Carolina and under the command of General Johnson Pettigrew. For decades North Carolina veterans felt slighted by the attention that Virginians received at Gettysburg. Although Pettigrew's men did not get across the stone wall as the Virginians did, the part of the wall they did reach was several yards past the Armistead marker. This was because they hit The Angle where it bent back from Cemetery Ridge. In 1986 they finally got their revenge when a monument commemorating the 26th North Carolina Infantry was placed several yards beyond the Armistead marker. While the 26th North Carolina did take part in Pickett's Charge and did suffer an exceedingly high casualty rate at Gettysburg,

One of many monuments erected by the Civil War veterans from New York State at Gettysburg. (Library of Congress)

there is little historical evidence supporting the placement of this monument. By most accounts, the 26th North Carolina was at least a hundred yards north of the spot the monument was placed. However, if the monument had been put in a more historically accurate spot, it would not have been in the proximity of the Armistead marker or near The Angle. In the opinion of Thomas Desjardin, a historian at Gettysburg, the North Carolina Monument Committee's main goal in placing the marker was to satisfy "their rivalry toward the Armistead marker."

Little Round Top:
Remembering Strong Vincent

Between the late 1870s when the first monument was placed on the Gettysburg battlefield, through the late 1880s when the majority of the monuments were erected, no veteran's group strove harder than the men from the 83rd Pennsylvania Infantry. Beginning with that first regimental marker placed in 1878, the 83rd Pennsylvania erected six separate monuments and markers on Little Round Top. All of these were designed to honor their fallen commander, Colonel Strong Vincent, who was killed leading the first wave of Union troops to reach Little Round Top. The man most responsible for these monuments was Oliver Norton, a bugler and flag bearer who was at Vincent's side when he was killed. The first marker, a marble slab placed on the spot where Vincent was killed, was followed by a plaque that was put up 10 years later and two hundred feet away that also was supposed to mark the spot Vincent was killed. The following year the 83rd Pennsylvania Regiment put up a monument of their own on Little Round Top. Despite the stipulation, by the

Pennsylvania State Monument Commission, prohibiting monuments representing common soldiers from resembling any particular commander, the statue commemorating the 83rd Pennsylvania was a dead ringer for Vincent, complete with his "unique and substantial sideburns." Nine years later Vincent's brigade also erected a monument on Little Round Top in his honor. However, Norton was still unsatisfied and petitioned for additional markers in 1910. This time to no avail.

Oliver Norton was also instrumental in the erection of the first statue on the Gettysburg battlefield in 1888. The statue honored the actions of General Gouverner K. Warren during the battle. It is now a commonly held belief that Warren saved the day by directing Union troops to the undefended Little Round Top when he discovered that it was being threatened by a Confederate attack on the second day of the Gettysburg battle. That belief is based on a single letter written by Warren in 1872, which describes the sun's reflection "glistening" off the guns and bayonets of the attacking Confederate force. Today, a larger-than-life bronze statue of Warren holding a pair of binoculars commemorates his action. Yet, there is a problem with Warren's account. Because of the time of day and the angle of the sun, it would have been impossible for him to have seen any kind of reflection coming from the direction of the Confederate attack. Indeed, there is an entirely different account from a signal officer who had also been on Little Round Top. According to this account, the signal officer had been trying to convince Warren of the impending attack, when a shell burst nearby, prompting the officer to exclaim, "Now do you see them?"

Monument honoring General Gouverner K. Warren, on Little Round Top. (Library of Congress)

Norton's success in erecting monuments for the 83rd Pennsylvania kindled a rivalry with veteran organizations from New York, as both states vied for dominance on the Gettysburg battlefield. Accordingly, the 44th New York Infantry erected a four-story "castle" on top of Little Round Top, which dwarfed the other markers on that part of the field. The New York Monument Commission didn't stop until every New York regiment and battery that had participated in the battle had its own monument. In addition, eight generals from New York were honored with monuments or statues. The commission erected another large monument, 13 feet high, which included depictions of New York generals not otherwise honored. Still not satisfied, the commission erected one final monument in 1925 called the New York Auxiliary Monument, for the units and commanders "not otherwise honored on this field." Not to be outdone, the state of Pennsylvania erected a 70-foot tall, cathedral-sized monument that included the name of every one of the 34,000 soldiers from Pennsylvania who served at Gettysburg. At a cost of $182,000, the monument featured seven life-size bronze statues and remains the most magnificent structure on the battlefield.

Little Round Top, a scene of major fighting during the battle of Gettysburg. (Library of Congress)

Longstreet's Revenge:
Southern Strategy at Gettysburg

One of the things that sets Gettysburg apart from most other Civil War battlefields is that the majority of the 1,400 monuments, statues, and markers were constructed by Northern states to commemorate the actions of Union soldiers and officers. The two most obvious reasons for this are that Gettysburg was the only major battle that took place on Northern soil and that Gettysburg was one of the few battles in the eastern theater that the North won. However, that doesn't explain why a battlefield visitor can tour the most famous parts of the battlefield without seeing any Confederate monuments. The reason for this is a decision made by John Bachelder during his tenure as the superintendent of the Gettysburg Battlefield Monument Association when it became apparent that a firm set of guidelines were needed to deal with the large number of monuments sprouting all over the Gettysburg battlefield. In 1887, Bachelder announced that regiments erecting monuments would be required to place them "on the line of battle." What this meant was that monuments could only be placed on the spot where a unit entered the fight. Because the Union army was on the defensive at Gettysburg, only Union units were deemed to have entered the fight at places where the fighting took place. The Confederate battle lines were as much as half a mile away, so they entered the fight a considerable distance from where the fighting took place. While this sounds confusing, what it ultimately meant was that Confederate units were not allowed to place monuments anywhere near The Angle or the crest of Little Round Top where the bulk of the fighting took place on July 2 and 3.

Another factor that contributed to the dearth of Confederate monuments was the lack of money available to Southern veteran organizations after the war. While the North enjoyed the effects of a growing industrialized society, the South was mired in rural poverty and Reconstruction. The money that was available was used to reinter the bodies of Confederate soldiers killed at Gettysburg in Southern graveyards. The Southern states decided to erect state monuments to commemorate all the soldiers who participated in the battle from each particular state. Thus, along the Confederate line of battle you have monuments from each state, in descending order of their participation and in descending grandeur, depending on the relative wealth and significance of each state—from the richly elaborate Virginia monument, featuring a larger-than-life Robert E. Lee on horseback, to the relatively modest Florida monument several miles away. Recent efforts to address the imbalance of monuments at Gettysburg have been mixed. While North Carolina was successful in its efforts to place a marker near The Angle, the recent efforts of Alabama to place a marker on Little Round Top have failed.

Until very recently, Robert E. Lee was the only Confederate general honored with a statue at Gettysburg. However, in 1998 Lee was joined by a monument commemorating his second-in-command, General James Longstreet. The Longstreet statue culminated a long struggle to rehabilitate Longstreet's post-Civil War reputation. Failure at Gettysburg hit the Army of Northern Virginia very hard because it was the first time they had tasted unequivocal defeat. The search for reasons for the defeat began almost as soon as the battle ended. Fearing that the battlefield defeat may have been God's will, the Confederate army underwent a massive religious revival. However, it wasn't long before the search for flesh and blood scapegoats began. First, attention was focused on General J.E.B. Stuart who had led his cavalry on a fruitless raid that caused them to miss the first two days of combat. Next, it was focused General Richard Ewell who had failed to attack Cemetery Hill late on the first day of battle as, some argued, Stonewall Jackson surely would have if he had still been alive. And finally, the Confederate defeat was laid at the feet of General Longstreet who, it was argued by some, had failed to carry out Lee's instructions and had acted too slowly.

The destruction of Longstreet's reputation began shortly after Lee's death, with the rise of the Lost Cause mythos. Led by the discredited General Jubal Early, a small coterie of disgruntled Confederate officers began a campaign based on the underlying theme that the North only won the Civil War because of superior resources and manpower. A central element of the theme was General Lee's infallibility. Thus, it was only logical to conclude that Lee's defeat at Gettysburg was the result of the failures of Lee's subordinates, because it could not have been caused by any failure of Lee. James Longstreet, who served as a general in the Confederate army from Bull Run to Appomattox and was promoted ahead of Stonewall Jackson as Lee's highest-ranking subordinate, made himself a perfect target for Early when he joined the Republican Party after the war and campaigned for General Grant in the 1868 presidential election. However, Longtreet's most provocative act, in the eyes of Early, was his annoying habit of actually assigning some culpability to Lee for Pickett's Charge and the Confederate defeat at Gettysburg.

At a time when almost every high-ranking Confederate military officer was being honored with statues and monuments and where all sorts of buildings and landmarks were being named after Confederate heroes, General Longstreet was all but forgotten. Until the Longstreet statue was put up in Gettysburg, only his home state of Georgia had remembered Longstreet by naming a small highway overpass in his honor. Longstreet's reputation began to improve after Michael Shaara published a fictional account of the battle in his Pulitzer Prize winning novel *The Killer Angels* in 1974. The Longstreet in *The Killer Angels* disagreed with Lee about attacking the Union Army at Gettysburg and patiently explained

Painting, by H.A. Ogden, of General James Longstreet at Gettysburg, who was scorned by the South after the war for criticizing General Lee. (Library of Congress)

to a visiting British officer exactly why Pickett's Charge was going to fail before it had begun. When Ted Turner decided to turn *The Killer Angels* into a motion picture, Shaara's sympathetic portrayal of Longstreet began to take hold. In the movie *Gettysburg*, actor Tom Berenger portrayed Longstreet as the voice of reason that counter-balanced Lee's almost apocalyptic vision of the battle. Several years after the movie, a private group inspired by this revised version of Longstreet raised enough money to commission a statue of him and received permission to place it at Gettysburg. The moderately sized statue differed greatly from earlier equestrian statues at Gettysburg, because it did not include a large pedestal. Instead, Longstreet is seated on a horse that is standing directly on the ground and forever guarding the park's picnic area.

Capital Connection:
Monuments in Richmond and Washington

While the South may have lost the monument battle at Gettysburg, most other major Civil War battlefields feature a healthy number of Confederate monuments. However, the place featuring the most Confederate monuments is not a battlefield—it is the old Confederate capital city of Richmond, Virginia. The city was well-known for its outdoor sculptures before the war and featured the only full-scale statue of George Washington. Created by Jean-Antoine Houdon, probably the greatest French sculptor of the era, the statue was placed in the rotunda of the Virginia State Capitol in 1796 and is said to be a near-perfect likeness of Washington.

The planning of a similar statue in honor of Robert E. Lee began shortly after his death in 1870. After much debate over the selection of a sculptor, the aptly named Jean Antoine Mercie was selected, and on May 31, 1890, the equestrian statue of Lee was dedicated on Monument Avenue. In the 20 years that followed, the Lee statue was joined along Monument Avenue by statues commemorat-

ing President Jefferson Davis, Stonewall Jackson, J.E.B. Stuart, and naval officer Matthew Fontaine Maury. In addition to the statues along Monument Avenue, several sculptural works have been erected in and around the Virginia state capitol. The most impressive of these is a life-size bronze statue of Robert E. Lee, which was placed directly on the spot where he stood on April 23, 1861 and accepted his commission to command troops from Virginia. Richmond also boasts monuments commemorating General A.P. Hill, the Richmond Howitzers, a Soldiers and Sailors Monument, and a 90-foot pyramid made of granite blocks in the Hollywood Cemetery. Placed near markers for J.E.B. Stuart, George Pickett, and Jefferson Davis, this monument commemorates the 18,000 Confederate soldiers buried in the cemetery.

Monument honoring General J.E.B. Stuart, one of many on Monument Avenue in Richmond, Virginia. (Library of Congress)

Not surprisingly, the city featuring the largest number of Civil War-era monuments is the Federal capital of Washington. There are no fewer than 41 statues featuring Union officers in the city. These include James Garfield, George Meade, Winfield Hancock, David Farragut, John Logan, George Thomas, James McPherson, William Sherman, John Rawlins, George McClellan, Phil Sheridan, and Phil Kearney. Ironically, there is also a statue commemorating a man who served as a Confederate general in Washington. However, the statue of Albert Pike, who commanded the Confederate Department of Indian Territory early in the war, has much more to do with his role as a leader of the Freemasons than with his nominal role as a Confederate military commander. Civil War memorials are also featured on both ends of the reflecting pool in the National Mall. The most famous of these is the Lincoln Memorial, dedicated long after the war, on May 30, 1922. The other Civil War statue, honoring General Ulysses Grant, features two almost life-size battle scenes flanking a larger-than-life equestrian statue of Grant himself. Washington is also the home of the Arsenal Monument, which honors 21 young women who were killed in a terrible explosion at the Washington Arsenal in 1864; The Nuns of the Battlefield, which honors the hundreds of women who served as nurses during the war; the Emancipation Monument, commemorating the freed men and women who contributed to the war effort; and the African-American Civil War Memorial, which features the only sculpture by an African-American artist on federal land in the city.

Monument honoring General Ulysses S. Grant, near the Reflecting Pool in Washington, D.C. (Library of Congress)

CHAPTER 13

CONTINUING CONTROVERSIES OF THE CIVIL WAR

Switched at Birth: The Last Prisoners of War

In 1906, the city fathers of York, Maine, signed a contract with J.O. Golbranson and Company to have Fred Barnicoat, an English sculptor living in nearby Quincy, Massachusetts, create a white granite statue honoring the town's Civil War veterans. When the statue was delivered however, it resembled "Johnny Reb" more than it did "Billy Yank." Unlike the myriad of other Civil War statues that inhabit town squares throughout New England, the city of York's statue had a slouch hat, a long beard, and a haversack. A local reporter investigating the phenomenon concluded that the artist's knowledge of the Civil War must have been "a little foggy." However, that seems unlikely, as Barnicoat also worked on an 85-foot-tall Confederate monument that ended up in Montgomery, Alabama. What is more likely is that J.O. Golbranson and Company, a firm which employed 25 men and did business throughout the country, mistakenly sent a statue designed for a Southern town. Why the people of York accepted the statue and put it up in the center of town remains a mystery. Years later, when they discovered that a small town in South Carolina had a similar problem, the citizens of York offered a "friendly exchange of our last two prisoners of war." However, the folks from Kingstree, South Carolina, weren't interested. They replied that they were quite happy with their "handsome Yankee friend."

While the story of how the York monument was erected without anyone realizing the error remains cloudy, more than 2,000 people showed up in 1910 for the dedication of the Civil War monument in Kingstree, South Carolina.

Confederate soldier monument mistakenly sent to York, Maine. (Library of Congress)

However, delivery of the $2,500 statue, which was commissioned by the United Daughters of the Confederacy, was delayed for unknown reasons. A month later, the South Carolina company that cut the granite statue delivered a figure with short hair and a trim mustache, wearing a regulation army kepi. Shortly after delivery, the statue was erected without ceremony. Although it is unlikely that the error escaped detection, once it was hoisted on top of its 32-foot-high pedestal, the "Confederate-Yankee" became an open secret in Kingstree.

A marble monument that was erected in Elberton, Georgia, which also closely resembled "Billy Yank," had a more troubled past. Created by Arthur Beter, an immigrant who had probably never seen a Confederate soldier, the 8-foot-high sculpture was unveiled in 1898 to almost universal derision. The "squatty mustachioed figure" was finally knocked off its pedestal on August 14, 1900 and buried in the town square. After it was replaced by a more conventional Confederate soldier monument, Beter's creation was all but forgotten for the next 80 years. In 1982, the statue was exhumed, cleaned off in a local car wash, and put back on display at the Elberton Granite Museum.

The Fabrication of a Legend: Abraham Lincoln's Birth Cabin

In 1876, more than $100,000 was collected for the construction of a memorial to honor President Abraham Lincoln. However, the harsh climate of postwar reconstruction stalled the project until 1911 when Congress passed legislation creating the Lincoln Memorial Commission. The cornerstone for the monument was finally laid in 1915, and the Lincoln Memorial was officially completed in 1922. (Ironically, the ceremony for the monument honoring the president who had ended slavery was interrupted by 21 African-Americans who left the dedication, to protest segregated seating arrangements.) While the politicians in Washington were dawdling, an entrepreneur from New York named Alfred Dennett decided to honor Lincoln in his own way. In 1895 he purchased Thomas Lincoln's old Sinking Springs Farm, hoping to turn it into a tourist attraction. Because the small cabin where Abraham Lincoln had been born had disappeared, Dennett bought a two-story cabin from a neighboring farm and used the best logs to build a cabin on the Lincoln farm. When questioned about the cabin's authenticity by a local newspaper reporter, Dennett replied, "One cabin is as good as another." Despite his efforts, few people were willing to travel to Hodgenville, Kentucky, to see this "historic structure," so Dennett decided to take the cabin on the road.

The first stop for the cabin was the Tennessee Centennial Exposition in 1897. To make the exhibit more attractive, Dennett purchased a second log cabin and dubbed it the birthplace of President Jefferson Davis. Both cabins traveled to Buffalo, New York, in 1901 for the Pan-American Exposition. This time Dennett added 150 black men and women, who were billed as former slaves living in the "genuine cabins in which Abraham Lincoln and Jefferson Davis were born." The next stop was Coney Island, but during shipping the logs for the cabins became intermingled. Once again, Dennett had a unique solution. The logs were combined into one large cabin called the Lincoln and Davis Cabin. After the exhibition, Dennett then sold the logs to Robert Collier, publisher of *Collier's Weekly*, who shipped them back to Kentucky. Collier reassembled the 'Lincoln and Davis' cabin in a park in Louisville, while collecting donations for the construction of a permanent home for his "historical structure." The Lincoln Farm Association raised more than $350,000 (mostly from school children) to construct a massive neoclassical temple—complete with a 56-step entrance—to house the cabin, and President Theodore Roosevelt was invited to lay the cornerstone in 1909. Two years later the massive building, which was designed by John Russell Pope, was finished. When Pope realized that the cabin was too large to fit inside, he cut several feet off its length and width.

The 12 x 17-foot Lincoln mini-cabin is now owned and displayed by the National Park Service, which still maintains the charade that the cabin was reconstructed

The non-birth cabin of President Abraham Lincoln in Hodgenville, Kentucky. (Library of Congress)

from "some of the original logs" found "on or very near" the Lincoln birth site. In addition to the cabin, a visitor can also gaze at the spot where an old oak tree had once grown. The tree, which died in 1976, served as a survey point for determining property lines and was supposedly the "last living link" to Abraham Lincoln. Apparently all claims that some of the logs in the cabin were once a part of Jefferson Davis's birthplace have been dropped. However, the Confederate president can rest comfortably as he has not been forgotten. In Davis's birthplace, Todd County, Kentucky, the world's tallest (351-foot) concrete obelisk was constructed in 1924. Although the Davis monument cost a lot less ($200,000) than the memorial in Hodgenville, it is home to a festival in which a new Miss Confederacy is crowned every year.

The Burning of Columbia: An Accident of War

On February 17, 1865, General William Tecumseh Sherman's army completed its 16-day march from Savannah, Georgia, to Columbia, South Carolina. While most men in Sherman's army thought that there would be a terrible battle for control of the city, by the time they arrived fewer than 500 Confederate cavalrymen remained to defend the state capital. During the march, Sherman had ordered the torching of several small towns, but upon his arrival in Columbia, he promised Mayor T.J. Goodwyn that, though he was obligated to destroy some government buildings, "not a finger's breath of your city shall be harmed." Three factors conspired to prevent Sherman from upholding his promise. The first was General Beauregard's order, three days earlier, to take all the cotton out of the warehouses in Columbia and put them in the street "to be carried out of town and burned." Unfortunately, in the general confusion of the evacuation, most of the highly flammable cotton bales were left behind in the streets. The second factor was the large amount of liquor that was being stored in the city. During the course of the war, the price of a gallon of whiskey had risen from $.25 to $25. As a result, residents of the city hoarded huge amounts of alcohol, which was freely distributed to Sherman's men when they advanced into Columbia. The casks of wine and liquor also added to the general conflagration once the fire started. Despite attempts to keep the men in check, new detachments brought in to replace drunken soldiers quickly joined the festivities themselves. Sherman commented on this afterward: "Whoever heard of an evacuated city to be left a depot of liquor for an army to occupy?" And finally, between 7 and 8 p.m., a gale-force wind hit the city, which blew southwest by west. The wind blew flakes of cotton throughout the city, reminding some "of a Northern snow-storm."

No one can say for certain what started the blaze that erupted in Columbia that night. Some attributed it to soldiers smoking cigars near the Trinity Episcopal Church, while others blame signal rockets that were fired every night by each corps in Sherman's army. However, once the fire started, there was little that could be done to contain it. One witness said that "in less than no time, it looked as though it rained fire from heaven." The fire continued to rage until the wind shifted back to the east. Lacking additional fuel, the fire burned itself out by morning. As a testament to how quickly the fire erupted and spread, between 150 and 200 Union soldiers burned to death during the night. After it was over, Sherman blamed Confederate General Wade Hampton for starting the fire by lighting bales of cotton, but admitted later that it was a lie. However, Sherman was adamant that his men did not deliberately burn Columbia. "If I had made up my mind to burn Columbia, I would have burnt it with no more feeling than I would a common prairie dog village, but I did not do it." Sherman's army remained in Columbia for three more days, and by the account of Chancellor James Parsons Carroll, "Not another dwelling was burned." According to the town official, "Perfect tranquillity prevailed throughout the town."

Today, the city of Columbia contains at least nine markers attributing the great fire solely to Sherman and his men. The idea that Union troops deliberately set the fire is compounded by a display in the South Carolina Confederate Relic Room and Museum that claims that "with no CSA troops to resist, General Sherman's men burned 80 percent of the city." According to historian James Loewen, this "may be the least accurate museum operated by a state government anywhere in the United States." In all, approximately 458 buildings burned in the fire. This amounted to one-third of the buildings in the city, and almost all of these were located in the city's business district. While it may be argued that Sherman lost control of his men and that some drunken soldiers may have started the fire, there is no evidence to suggest that Sherman ordered the firing of the city or desired that it be burned. In fact, an international tribunal was established in 1871 to investigate British claims of assets lost in the fire. After several days of testimony, the commission concluded that the fire was "an accident of war."

Black Confederates:
A Modern-Day Phenomenon

Darlington, South Carolina, best known for the Darlington Raceway, is also the home of Henry "Dad" Brown, the most famous drummer to serve in the Confederate army. Today, there are at least four markers in Darlington that honor Brown's service during the Civil War. The first marker was put up in 1907, at his grave site, and the latest was a roadside marker, dedicated in 2001. Although Brown's primary claim to fame was that he was a black man who served in the Confederate army, by all accounts he was a remarkable figure. He managed to free himself from bondage, learned to read and write at a time when it was illegal for him to do so, and served as a drummer in three separate wars. In addition to Brown, there are also 10 or 12 other African-American men from Darlington who served in the Confederate army in some capacity and succeeded in drawing pensions after the war. (From 1919 to 1925, South Carolina granted pensions to Confederate veterans and widows.) Although many Confederate officers brought along slaves with them

Stonewall Jackson's cook during the Civil War—one of the roles blacks were allowed to hold in the Confederate army. (Library of Congress)

to serve as cooks and servants, the Confederate government did not officially recognize their service until February 17, 1864, when the Confederate Congress passed a law designed to "increase the efficiency of the Army by the employment of free Negroes and slaves in certain capacities." These capacities included such things as "teamsters, cooks, musicians, nurses, hospital attendants, blacksmiths, hostlers, foragers and wheelwrights." Slaves did not get paid, but free blacks who served with the army were paid the same rate as privates. When the Army of Northern Virginia surrendered at Appomattox in April 1865, 36 black men were with the army and given official paroles from the U.S. government. They included cooks, teamsters, musicians, and servants.

The markers commemorating Henry Brown are not unique. There are at least a dozen other monuments and markers in various states pertaining to black Confederates, and more are appearing on a regular basis. A marker honoring an unknown Confederate "negro servant" was put up recently outside the Walker Top Church in South Mountains State Park, in North Carolina. Perhaps the largest monument of this sort is in Canton, Mississippi, where a 21-foot obelisk was erected in honor of 14-year-old Willis Howcott. According to the monument, Willis was killed during combat in 1865, and it describes Howcott as being "a colored boy of rare loyalty and faithfulness."

During the war—according to historian Robert Krick, who has studied the records of more than 150,000 Confederate soldiers—less than a dozen African-Americans actually served in combat (although approximately 179,000 African-Americans served in the Union Army). One of those who did was Holt Collier. He was honored with a headstone, placed on his grave in Greenville, Mississippi, on February 28, 2004. According to the marker, Collier served as a "sharpshooter and cavalryman" in Company I of the Ninth Texas Brigade. Collier, who was born in 1846 and belonged to Howell Hinds, went to war with his owner and master in 1861. After the war Collier gained notoriety when he served as a guide on a bear hunt for Theodore Roosevelt in 1903. According to Roosevelt: "He was a man of sixty and could neither read nor write, but he had all the dignity of an African chief.... In the Civil War he had not only followed his master to battle as his body-servant, but had acted under him as sharpshooter against the Union soldiers." Collier succeeded in finding a bear for Roosevelt to shoot, but because the bear was tied up, Roosevelt abstained.

A photograph of Holt Collier taken by Alexander Lambert in 1903. Collier served as a sharpshooter during the Civil War. (Library of Congress

The idea of allowing slaves to enter the Confederate army was first brought up by General Patrick Cleburne, in a letter written on January 2, 1864 and signed by 13 other Confederate officers. The reason, according to Cleburne, "was that slavery [had] become a military weakness." Because the Union was proposing to arm and equip 100,000 freed slaves as Union soldiers, Cleburne felt that it was necessary for the Confederacy to beat them to the punch. "We can do this more effectually than the North can now do, for we can give the negro not only his own freedom, but that of his wife and child, and can secure it to him in his old home." Cleburne was also confident that freed slaves would fight. "If...they can be made to face and fight bravely against their former masters, how much more probable is it that with the allurement of a higher reward, and led by those masters, they would submit to discipline and face dangers." However, President Jefferson Davis did not agree. In fact, Davis thought the idea so inflammatory that he decided the "best policy under the circumstances [was] to avoid all publicity." The idea was resurrected late in the war when the Confederate Congress narrowly passed a resolution authorizing the recruitment of African-American companies. Several companies did begin drilling in Richmond, Virginia, but the war ended before they could be deployed. Even at this late date, the idea of arming African-Americans and allowing them into the Confederate army was controversial. Perhaps Howell Cobb, a politician from Georgia, said it best: "If slaves will make good soldiers, our whole theory of slavery is wrong."

When Things Go Wrong:
The Mass Hangings of 1862

President Abraham Lincoln ordered the largest mass hanging on a single day in American history on December 26, 1862. On that day, 38 Native Americans of the Dakota (Sioux) tribe were hung in Mankato, Minnesota, for their role in sacking the town of New Ulm four months earlier. A monument made of solid granite and weighing more than 200 pounds was erected in 1912 to mark the spot of the mass hanging. The inscription on the marker was curt, and read in bold block letters: "Here Were Hanged thirty-eight Sioux Indians." After years of controversy, the marker was taken down in 1972 and is now supposedly being held "in protective custody" at an undisclosed location. Five years later, a 35-ton Buffalo Statue was erected near the spot where the hangings occurred, in what is now called Reconciliation Park. However, there is no indication on the statue or in the small, pocket-sized park of what occured there in 1862.

Incredibly, the mass hanging in Mankato could have been much worse. In a period of six weeks, the military commission appointed by General John Pope to investigate the uprising conducted 392 separate trials. These trials were less than fair, as Pope announced his intentions quite clearly. "It is my purpose utterly to exterminate the Sioux if I have the power to do so.... Destroy everything belonging to them, and force them out to the plains....They are to be treated as maniacs or wild beasts." One of the prosecution's best witnesses was a black man named Godfrey, who testified in exchange for a commutation of his own sentence of death by hanging for participating in the attacks. According to Isaac Heard, the official court recorder of the trials, "Godfrey was the means of bringing to justice a large number of the savages.... Such an Indian had a double barreled gun, another a single barreled, another a long one, another a short one, another a lance.... Not the least thing had escaped his eye or ear." By the time the list was sent to President Lincoln for his authorization, it contained 303 names. Lincoln quickly decided that it would not be a good idea to hang such a large number of men and asked for the complete records to be sent to Washington.

When President Lincoln returned the list to General Pope, it contained only 39 names. One man (Tatehmihma) was given a reprieve on the day of the hanging, but the rest were marched to a specially built scaffold at precisely 10 a.m. The *St. Paul Pioneer Press* reported what happened next:

> Three slow, measured, and distinct beats on the drum by Major Brown..., and the rope was cut by Mr. Duly. The scaffold fell, and thirty-eight lifeless bodies were left dangling between heaven and earth. As the platform fell, there was one, not loud, but prolonged cheer from the soldiery and citizens who were spectators, and then all were quiet and earnest witnesses of the scene.

To add further insult to the deaths, the 38 bodies were thrown onto a sandbar in the Minnesota River, and doctors from all over gathered to claim them for medical research. To speed the process, each doctor was given a number and assigned a particular corpse. The only doctor given the special privilege of choosing his own corpse was Dr. William Mayo, who had helped treat the wounded at New Ulm. (Dr. Mayo's sons William and Charles went on to form the Mayo Clinic.) To date, only one set of remains has been returned to the Dakota tribe for a proper burial.

There was another mass hanging in 1862 that claimed, all together, even more lives than the episode in Mankato, Minnesota. On October 1, 1862, Confederate irregular militia, led by Colonel William C. Young, rounded up more than 200 men in and around Cooke County, Texas, who were alleged to be Union sympathizers. The vast majority of residents in Northern Texas were small farmers, and the residents of the county had voted overwhelmingly against the secession referendum. The crime these men had committed was signing a petition protesting the exemption given to slave owners in the Conscription Act passed by the Confederate Congress in April 1862. Of the men arrested, 70 were locked up in a vacant store on the courthouse square in Gainesville, Texas. Colonel Young, one of the largest slave owners in the county, then organized a "citizen's court" of 12 jurors and ordered that only a majority vote was needed to convict the prisoners. Seven of the most influential leaders were quickly convicted and hung, but then an angry mob took over and lynched 14 more before order could be restored. A few days

Lithograph depicting the terrible scenes that occurred in Texas in 1862, taken from sketches by Frederick Sumner, who was a leader of the Unionists in that state during the Civil War. (Library of Congress)

later, Colonel Young was killed by an unknown assassin, and the decision to release the remaining prisoners was reversed. In quick order, 19 more men were convicted and hung over the course of the week. A total of 41 men were hung, although two others were shot and killed as they tried to escape.

John Crisp, a local blacksmith, was one of those put on trial. The man who testified against Crisp was Dr. Eli Thomas. According to Dr. Thomas, "John M. Crisp swore me into a secret organization having for its object the reconstruction of the old Constitution and Union. He gave me the sign, grip, and password." Crisp was found guilty and hung and, despite his testimony, Dr. Thomas was hung as well. There is a historical marker near the courthouse, commemorating the "Great Hanging at Gainesville," which says in part: "At a meeting of Cooke County citizens...it was unanimously resolved to establish a citizen's court..., 68 men were brought speedily before the court...39 of them were found guilty of conspiracy and insurrection, sentenced, and immediately hanged." (Two were found to be deserters and tried before a military tribunal before they were hung.) The bodies, unclaimed by family members too frightened to come forward, were buried in a mass grave. What the marker, erected in 1964, doesn't include is that Confederate authorities did nothing to stop the violence or to punish those who took part in it. (One man from Denton, Texas, was convicted after the war.) Other hangings occurred in nearby Wise, Grayson, and Denton, counties and historian Richard Brown estimates that as many as 171 pro-Union people were killed in North Texas during the war. When a company of soldiers from North Texas, serving in nearby Arkansas, learned what had happened in Gainesville, they almost mutinied. Only the firm hand of General Joseph Shelby prevented the men from returning to Gainesville to exact revenge for the killings.

CHAPTER 14

THE CIVIL WAR
IN POETRY

Thomas Read: Sheridan's Wild Ride

General Philip Sheridan's early life was as obscure as his later life was celebrated. Born in 1831, somewhere between County Cavan, Ireland, and Somerset, Ohio, Sheridan is most commonly thought of as being born while his family was traveling through the city of Albany, New York. An 1853 graduate of the West Point Military Academy (after serving a year's suspension for assaulting a cadet sergeant), Sheridan proved so adept as a quartermaster that he was one of the very few West Point graduates who could not get himself promoted early in the war. While most of his contemporaries were commanding troops in battle as colonels and generals, Sheridan languished as a captain and quartermaster for General Halleck's headquarters in Corinth, Mississippi. It wasn't until his friend Colonel Gordon Granger was promoted to command the Cavalry Corps of the Army of the Mississippi, in March 1862, that Sheridan got his chance. Promoted by his friend Granger to colonel of the Second Michigan Cavalry, Sheridan was finally able to enter the fray. He quickly distinguished himself as a leader and a cavalryman and was promoted 35 days later to brigadier general and given command of a division in the Army of the Ohio. Being one of the few generals who survived the Union disaster at Chickamauga with his reputation intact, Sheridan led the impromptu and improbably successful Union charge up Missionary Ridge a few weeks later. Sheridan's career was given another boost by General Ulysses Grant, who had witnessed the charge and who subsequently chose Sheridan as commander of the Cavalry Corps of the Army of the Potomac.

Although they had not met prior to the victory at Missionary Ridge, the feisty Sheridan, who had been described by his previous commander as "worth his weight in gold," got along very well with General Grant. Both men were of humble origins, short of stature, and very aggressive on the field of battle. Unlike most generals in the Army of the Potomac, who worried about what the Confederate army would do next, both Grant and Sheridan only worried about what they would do next. After Grant's army was bloodied at the battle of the Wilderness, Sheridan convinced Grant to let him go directly after General J.E.B. Stuart's cavalry. Leading 10,000 blue troopers in a column 13 miles long, Sheridan easily defeated the overmatched and outmanned Confederate cavalry in a battle at Yellow Tavern, which resulted in Stuart's own death. When the city of Washington was threatened by General Jubal Early's army a few months later, Grant again turned to Sheridan. After defeating Early at Winchester, Fisher's Hill, and Tom's Brook, Sheridan believed that he had defeated Early and successfully disposed of the Confederate threat in the Shenandoah Valley.

Anxious to discuss his next assignment, "Little Phil" Sheridan left Winchester, Virginia, for a meeting in Washington with Secretary of War Stanton and President Lincoln on October 16, 1864. General Grant was eager to have Sheridan advance to Culpepper and Gordonsville, to threaten Richmond from the west. However, before Sheridan could reach his destination, he learned that General Early had surprised his army at Cedar Creek. Riding as quickly as he could, Sheridan retraced his steps and rejoined his army in time to turn the tables on Early and earn a spectacular Union victory. Sheridan made his rapid return aboard a horse named Rienzi that he had acquired shortly after he had been given his first combat command in Mississippi. Named after a nearby town, Rienzi stood more than 17 hands high and had tremendous strength and endurance. By war's end, Rienzi had participated in 19 battles and had been wounded several times.

A few weeks after the battle ended, a popular poet named Thomas Read wrote a poem in honor of Sheridan and his now famous horse. Read had become familiar with both Sheridan and Rienzi during a stay at Union headquarters near Murfreesboro, Tennessee, as a guest of General Rosecrans earlier in the war. Read was given the idea of writing the poem by James Murdoch, a popular actor and "elocutionist." Murdoch had visited the Union headquarters in Chattanooga, Tennessee, after the battle of Missionary Ridge in search of his wounded son. When he learned that his son, who had served under Sheridan, had been killed and that the spot where he was buried was still controlled by the Confederates, he decided to stay until the body could be retrieved. During his stay, Murdoch would frequently entertain the troops by reciting poems around headquarters. Murdoch asked Read to write a poem commemorating Sheridan's ride that he could recite at a fair in Cincinnati to raise money for the war effort. When the day came for the recital, Murdoch was dismayed to find that Read had not yet even begun to write the piece. Murdoch quickly pulled out a copy of the latest *Harper's Weekly*, which had an account of the battle, and gave it to Read. An hour later, Read returned with "Sheridan's Ride."

Read, who was also an artist, created 17 different paintings depicting "Sheridan's Ride," which were quickly turned into colored lithographic prints and sold throughout the North. The poem became so famous that students were required to learn it by heart and recite it at school programs. For his part, Sheridan liked the poem, but changed Rienzi's name to Winchester when he realized that the horse had become more popular than the rider. In fact, Rienzi was so popular that, according to accounts of the day, the famous horse died in nine different states and was buried in 13 different styles. Phil Sheridan was either totally distraught when Rienzi died and "wept like a child," or he "patted the old cuss and walked off." After Rienzi/Winchester finally died for real, Sheridan had him stuffed and put him on display in the Army Museum in New York City. When the museum burned down in 1922, Rienzi was saved and given an army escort to the Smithsonian, where he now occupies a glass case in the Hall of Armed Forces History.

Sheridan's Ride
By Thomas Read

Up from the South at break of day,
Bringing to Winchester fresh dismay,
The affrighted air with a shudder bore,
Like a herald in haste, to the chieftain's door,
The terrible grumble and rumble and roar,
Telling the battle was on once more,
And Sheridan twenty miles away.

And wilder still those billows of war
Thundered along the horizon's bar,
And louder yet into Winchester rolled
The roar of that red sea uncontrolled,
Making the blood of the listener cold
As he thought of the stake in that fiery fray,
And Sheridan twenty miles away.

But there is a road from Winchester town,
A good, broad highway leading down;
And there through the flash of the morning light,
A steed as black as the steeds of night,
Was seen to pass as with eagle's flight —
As if he knew the terrible need,
He stretched away with the utmost speed;
Hills rose and fell—but his heart was gay,
With Sheridan fifteen miles away.

Still sprung from these swift hoofs, thundering South,
The dust, like the smoke from the cannon's mouth,
Or the trail of a comet sweeping faster and faster,
Foreboding to traitors the doom of disaster;
The heart of the steed and the heart of the master,
Were beating like prisoners assaulting their walls,
Impatient to be where the battle-field calls;
Every nerve of the charger was strained to full play,
With Sheridan only ten miles away.

Under his spurning feet the road
Like an arrowy Alpine river flowed;
And the landscape sped away behind
Like an ocean flying before the wind.
And the steed, like a bark fed with furnace ire,
Swept on with his wild eyes full of fire,
But lo! he is nearing his heart's desire—
He is snuffing the smoke of the roaring fray,
With Sheridan only five miles away.

The first that the General saw were the groups
Of stragglers, and then the retreating troops;
What was done—what to do—a glance told him both,
And striking his spurs with a terrible oath,
He dashed down the line 'mid a storm of huzzahs,
And the wave of retreat checked its course there because
The sight of the master compelled it to pause.

With foam and with dust the black charger was gray,
By the flash of his eye, and his red nostrils' play,
He seemed to the whole great army to say,
"I have brought you Sheridan all the way
From Winchester down to save the day!"
Hurrah, hurrah for Sheridan!
Hurrah, hurrah for horse and man!

And when their statues are placed on high
Under the dome of the Union sky—
The American soldiers' Temple of Fame—
There with the glorious General's name
Be it said in letters both bold and bright:
"Here is the steed that saved the day
By carrying Sheridan into the fight,
From Winchester—twenty miles away!"

Lithograph based on the poem by Thomas Read, depicting the famous ride of General Phil Sheridan and his horse Rienzi. (Library of Congress)

John Reuben Thompson:
Dead Soldier Poems

While the poem "Sheridan's Ride" inspired numerous paintings, the process also worked the other way around. In 1862, the *Southern Literary Messenger* published a poem by John Reuben Thompson describing the death and burial of a cavalry officer killed during General Stuart's first ride around the Union army. Stuart and his men broke camp very early on the morning of June 13, 1862, with orders from General Lee to find the right flank of General George McClellan's Union army. Stuart's troopers crossed the Totopotomy River at a bridge near Linney's Corner around 9:00 in the morning. When they ran into a small force of Union cavalrymen guarding the road, Stuart gave the order to "form fours, draw sabers, [and] charge." Captain William Latane, commanding the Essex Light Dragoons, led the charge. Before the war, the 29-year-old Latane had been a physician. He graduated from the Richmond Medical Academy in 1853 and took postgraduate courses the following year in Philadelphia before returning to his home near Richmond to practice medicine and manage the family plantation. All the Union cavalrymen took flight before Latane and his men could reach them, except for their commander, Captain William Royall. Latane charged Royall and slashed him with his saber, but Royall returned fire with his pistol. Latane was hit by two pistol shots and, by all accounts, was dead before his body hit the ground.

Latane's body was recovered by his brother John and placed in an ox-drawn cart. Because they were in enemy-held territory and traveling too fast to bring the body with them, John Latane brought the body to a nearby plantation called Westwood. There Catherine Brockenbrough, who lived at Westwood, and Mrs. Willoughby Newton of nearby Summer Hill promised John Latane that they would give his brother a proper funeral. Unable to find a clergyman, Mrs. Newton presided over the service that was attended by a small group of local women and children. (The exact location where Latane was buried is unknown, but in the 1920s, the Battlefield Markers Association placed a marker on privately held land on Summer Hill.) Two weeks later William Latane's fiancée, Martha Davis, wrote a letter to John Thompson, a poet and former editor of the *Southern Literary Messenger*, asking that he compose a poem in honor of Latane. When Thompson published "The Burial of Latane," it became an instant classic. Two years later, painter William D. Washington, who specialized in historical subjects and portraits, set up a studio in Richmond and began work on a painting depicting Letane's burial. Washington used members of a local literary group—some of the city's most prominent matrons and their maids—as models. After several months of work, Washington displayed his work at a gathering that "drew throngs of visitors." The painting was eventually made available as a relatively cheap lithograph and became a leading symbol in the mythology of the "Lost Cause."

The Burial of Latane
By John Reuben Thompson

The combat ranged not long, but ours the day;
And through the hosts that compassed us around
Our little band rode proudly on its way,
Leaving one gallant comrade, glory-crowned,
Unburied on the field he died to gain,
Single of all his men amid the hostile slain.

One moment on the battle's edge he stood,
Hope's halo like a helmet round his hair,
The next beheld him, dabbled in his blood,
Prostrate in death, and yet in death how fair!
Even thus he passed through the red gate of strife,
From earthly crowns and palms to an immortal life.

A brother bore his body from the field
And gave it unto stranger's hands that closed
The calm, blue eyes on earth forever sealed,
And tenderly the slender limbs composed:
Strangers, yet sisters, who with Mary's love,
Sat by the open tomb and weeping looked above.

A little child strewed roses on his bier,
Pale roses, not more stainless than his soul.
Nor yet more fragrant than his life sincere
That blossomed with good actions, brief, but whole:
The aged matron and the faithful slave
Approached with reverent feet the hero's lowly grave.

No man of God might say the burial rite
Above the "rebel"—thus declared the foe
That blanched before him in the deadly fight.
But woman's voice, in accents soft and low,
Trembling with pity, touched with pathos, read
Over his hallowed dust the ritual for the dead.

"'Tis sown in weakness, it is raised in power,"
Softly the promise floated on the air,
And the sweet breathings of the sunset hour
Came back responsive to the mourner's prayer;
Gently they laid him underneath the sod,
And left him with his fame, his country, and his God.

Let us not weep for him whose deeds endure,
So young, so brave, so beautiful, he died;
As he had wished to die; the past is sure,
Whatever yet of sorrow may betide
Those who still linger by the stormy shore,
Change cannot harm him now nor fortune touch him more.

And when Virginia, leaning on her spear,
Victrix et Vidua; the conflict done,
Shall raise her mailed hand to wipe the tear
That starts, as she recalls each martyred son,
No prouder memory her breast shall sway,
Than thine, our early-lost, lamented Latane.

Steel engraving taken from the painting The Burial of Latane, *by William Washington. (Library of Congress)*

Paul Hamilton Hayne:
Poet Laureate of the South

Very early in the war, patriotic poems, such as "The Burial of Latane," that dealt with the death of ordinary soldiers far from home—sometimes called "dying soldier" poems—became extremely popular in both the North and the South. This outpouring of sentimental literature served as a buffer against a war that was growing more and more gruesome. Oliver Wendell Holmes commented on this phenomenon in a lecture he gave in 1865: "There is a simple and genuine pathos in many of them. I do not know whether it sounds scholarly and critical and all the rest, but I think there is more nature and feeling in some of these [poems] than in very many poems of far higher pretensions and more distinguished origin." According to social historian Alice Fahs, "Dying soldier poems did not so much deny the deaths of soldiers as perform the difficult cultural task of making often anonymous deaths meaningful."

Perhaps the most renowned Southern poet of the era was Paul Hamilton Hayne, sometimes called the Laureate of the South. Hayne's father, a naval officer, died when he was very young, and Hayne was raised in Charleston, South Carolina, by an aristocratic uncle. Although he was trained as a lawyer, Hayne "had inherited the prestige of a noble name, high position, and a sufficient amount of wealth" and was free to follow his literary interests. In addition to writing poetry, Hayne served as the editor for the *Charleston Literary Gazette* and, with his two closest literary companions, Henry Timrod and William Gilmore Simms, started publication of a literary magazine. As was befitting a member of Charleston's high society, Hayne married Mary Middleton Michel, a "South Carolina lady of good English and Scotch descent." She was the daughter of an eminent French physician who had been awarded a gold medal by Napoleon for his services at the battle of Leipzig. As a resident of Charleston, Hayne was present when the war began with the firing on Fort Sumter, but his health was too delicate for him to join the military so he became a staff aide for Governor Francis Pickens.

Although the Civil War started in Charleston, the city seemed to escape most of the horrors of war. The blockading Union navy maintained a presence off Charleston Harbor, but the forts that ringed the city and its nearby islands provided protection for the residents of the city. On April 7, 1863, Hayne and his fellow Charlestonians got a front row seat when nine Union ironclads steamed into the harbor and attacked Fort Sumter. The attack was a dismal failure, as converging Confederate fire poured more than 2,000 shots on the Union vessels and secured approximately 400 hits before driving the gunboats away. Unable to take Fort Sumter by sea, the Union army focused its attention on nearby Morris Island. After weeks of steady bombardment and a fruitless and bloody frontal charge, Union commander Quincy Gillmore tried a more unconventional approach. He ordered the construction of a battery close enough to throw shells on the city of Charleston. After the 8-inch Parrott rifle, dubbed the Swamp Angel, was in place, Gillmore sent word that, unless Fort Sumter and Battery Wagner (on Morris Island) were immediately evacuated, he would bombard the city. General Beauregard protested Gillmore's threat to a city filled with "sleeping women and children," but refused to evacuate the two forts. At midnight on the night of August 22, 1863, the Swamp Angel began lobbing shells into the city.

While this was not the first time an army had shelled an enemy-defended city, it was the first time the shelling of civilians was used in an attempt to achieve military gain. To make matters worse, Gillmore had his men use special incendiary shells in an attempt to set fire to the city. Fortunately for the residents of Charleston, after 36 shots, the Swamp Angel exploded and most of the incendiary shells failed to ignite any fires of consequence in the city. Despite the intermittent shelling, most of the people in Charleston went about their daily affairs. However, Paul Hayne was not so lucky—his home and personal library were burned to the ground. He attempted to save some of the family silver and other personal possessions, but they were also lost when General Sherman's army captured the city late in the war. In 1866, the nearly destitute Hayne moved his family to a plot of land outside Augusta, Georgia, built a rude farmhouse, and lived as a recluse for the remaining

15 years of his life. The poems of Hayne received strong reviews and were very popular during his lifetime, but they have faded away over time, like the Southern aristocratic culture they represented.

Charleston at the Close of 1863
By Paul Hamilton Hayne

WHAT! Still does the mother of treason uprear
Her crest 'gainst the furies that darken her sea,
Unquelled by mistrust, and unblanched by a fear,
Unbowed her proud head, and unbending her knee,
Calm, steadfast and free!

Ay! launch your red lightnings! blaspheme in your wrath!
Shock earth, wave, and heaven with the blasts of your ire;
But she seizes your death-bolts yet hot from their path,
And hurls back your lightnings and mocks at the fire
Of your fruitless desire!

Ringed round by her brave, a fierce circlet of flame
Flashes up from the sword-points that cover her breast;
She is guarded by love, and enhaloed by fame,
And never, we swear, shall your footsteps be pressed,
Where her dead heroes rest.

Her voice shook the tyrant, sublime from her tongue
Fell the accents of warning! a prophetess grand—
On her soil the first life notes of liberty rung,
And the first stalwart blow of her gauntleted hand
Broke the sleep of her land.

What more? she hath grasped in her iron-bound will
The fate that would trample her honors to earth;
The light in those deep eyes is luminous still
With the warmth of her valor, the glow of her worth,
Which illumine the earth.

And beside her a knight the great Bayard had loved,
"Without fear or reproach," lifts her banner on high;
He stands in the vanguard majestic, unmoved,
And a thousand firm souls when that chieftain is nigh,
Vow "'tis easy to die!"

Their words have gone forth on the fetterless air,
The world's breath is hushed at the conflict! Before
Gleams the bright form of Freedom, with wreaths in her hair—
And what though the chaplet be crimsoned with gore—
We shall prize her the more!

And while Freedom lures on with her passionate eyes
To the height of her promise, the voices of yore
From the storied profound of past ages arise,
And the pomps of their magical music outpour
O'er the war-beaten shore!

Then gird your brave empress, O heroes! with flame,
Flashed up from the sword-points that cover her breast!
She is guarded by Love and enhaloed by Fame.
And never, stern foe! shall your footsteps be pressed
Where her dead martyrs rest!

Wreckage of the Swamp Angel, the 8-inch Parrott rifle that was used to shell Charleston, South Carolina, in 1863. (Library of Congress)

Walt Whitman: Union Nurse, American Poet

One of the poets who emerged during the Civil War but who has not faded into obscurity is Walt Whitman. While working as a journalist for the *Brooklyn Freeman*, Whitman began writing a group of poems he called *Leaves of Grass*. Unable to find a publisher, Whitman paid for the first printing of 795 copies out of his own pocket. When war broke out Whitman watched as two of his brothers rushed to join the army. Whitman, who was in his 40s, did not enlist. (He also had three other brothers who did not enlist: Jesse was committed to an insane asylum in 1864, Eddy was mentally handicapped and unfit for service, and Jeff was exempted as the family's main bread winner.) Of the two brothers who did enlist, Andrew contracted tuberculosis and soon died, but George Whitman enjoyed a distinguished career in the military. It was George's wounding at the battle of Fredericksburg that drew Walt Whitman to the battlefield. Relieved to discover that George had suffered only a superficial wound, Walt was shocked when he discovered the horrors of a Civil War battlefield. Outside of one field hospital, Whitman came upon "a heap of amputated feet, legs, arms, hands, &c., a full load for a one-horse cart." They were, he wrote in his journal, "human fragments, cut, bloody, black and blue, swelled and sickening." He stayed on for another 10 days to help out in the hospital, and then followed the wounded soldiers back to

Poet Walt Whitman served as a nurse during the Civil War. (National Archives)

Washington. For the next three years, Whitman spent the bulk of his time and money caring for wounded soldiers in the hospitals of Washington.

The Armory Square Hospital, where Whitman spent the bulk of his time, was located on ground that is now the National Air and Space Museum. Whitman explained why he went there, in a letter to his mother: "I devote myself much to Armory Square Hospital because it contains by far the worst cases, most repulsive wounds, has the most suffering & most need of consolation— I go every day without fail, & often at night—sometimes stay very late." From August 1861 to January 1865, Armory Square recorded the largest number of deaths of any Washington military hospital. To make matters worse, the hospital was next to a canal that served as an open sewer which was "filled with floating dead cats, all kinds of putridity, and reeking with pestilential odors." In fact, the water supply was so bad that medical treatment at the hospital may have killed as many patients

as it saved. It didn't help that the United States was still in the Dark Ages as far as medicine was concerned. Although thermometers were being used throughout France, there were only 20 thermometers in the entire Union army. A stethoscope was still seen as a novelty item, and many surgeons still "dusted" wounds with morphine rather than injecting the drug with a hypodermic needle.

Despite all the privations, Whitman and the other nurses performed an invaluable service. In a letter to a friend, Whitman noted that, "The doctors tell me I supply the patients with a medicine which all their drugs & bottles & powders are helpless to yield." In all, Whitman made more than 600 hospital trips and helped treat approximately 80,000 wounded men. One favorite of Whitman's was Private Lewis Brown, who suffered from a gunshot wound to his left

Poet Walt Whitman in later life. (Library of Congress)

leg. Brown remained in the hospital for two years because the leg, which was amputated five inches below the knee, wouldn't heal. Whitman spent many nights next to Brown's cot and they remained good friends after the war. Brown eventually outlived three wives and raised a son who became a lieutenant colonel in the Marine Corps.

During his time as a nurse, Whitman also worked on his series of poems he called *Drum Taps*, which was published early in 1865. However, after President Lincoln was assassinated, Whitman quickly wrote *Sequel to Drum Taps*, which included his best-known poem, "O Captain! My Captain!" The poems Whitman wrote were not about battles, but about the consequences of battles. He wrote about "the moonlight illuminating the dead on the battlefields, the churches turned into hospitals, the experience of dressing wounds..., and the trauma of battle nightmares for soldiers." Most critics savaged Whitman's war poems. The *New York Times* wrote that Whitman had "no ear...and no sense of the melody of verse." However, many of his fellow artists thought it a masterpiece. John Burroughs described it as "entirely new in modern literature." Eventually *Drum Taps* and *Sequel to Drum Taps* emerged as some of the most touching poems ever written about the experience of war. A stroke slowed Whitman down in 1873, but he continued to write until his death in 1892. Today he is know as the father of free verse and "the most original and passionate American poet."

Oh Captain! My Captain! By Walt Whitman

O Captain! my Captain! our fearful trip is done,
The ship has weather'd every rack, the prize we sought is won,
The port is near, the bells I hear, the people all exulting,
While follow eyes the steady keel, the vessel grim and daring;
But O heart! heart! heart!
O the bleeding drops of red,
Where on the deck my Captain lies,
Fallen cold and dead.

O Captain! my Captain! rise up and hear the bells;
Rise up—for you the flag is flung—for you the bugle trills,
For you bouquets and ribbon'd wreaths—for you the shores a-crowding,
For you they call, the swaying mass, their eager faces turning;
Here Captain! dear father!
This arm beneath your head!
It is some dream that on the deck,
You've fallen cold and dead.

My Captain does not answer, his lips are pale and still,
My father does not feel my arm, he has no pulse nor will,
The ship is anchor'd safe and sound, its voyage closed and done,
From fearful trip the victor ship comes in with object won;
Exult O shores, and ring O bells!
But I with mournful tread,
Walk the deck my Captain lies,
Fallen cold and dead.

BIBLIOGRAPHY

Adams, George. *General William S. Harney: Prince of Dragoons*. Lincoln, Nebr.: University of Nebraska Press, 2001.

Barrow, Charles Kelly, ed. *Black Confederates: An Anthology About Black Southerners*. Gretna, La.: Pelican Publishing Company, 2001.

Belden, Henry M. *Ballads and Songs*. Columbia, Mo.: University of Missouri Press, 1973.

Boatner, Mark M. *The Civil War Dictionary*. New York: David McKay Co., 1959.

Brummer, Sidney David. *Political History of New York State During the Civil War*. New York: AMS Press, Inc., 1967.

Calkins, Christopher. "From Petersburg to Appomattox April 2-9, 1865." Farmville, Va.: *The Farmville Herald*, 1993.

Catton, Bruce. *Never Call Retreat*. Garden City, N.Y.: Doubleday and Co., 1965.

———. *Terrible Swift Sword*. Garden City, N.Y.: Doubleday and Co., 1963.

Clark, James. *Recollections of James Lemuel Clark: Including Previously Unpublished Material on the Great Hanging at Gainsville, Texas in October 1862*. College Station, Tex.: Texas A&M Press, 2000.

Colton, Ray. *The Civil War in the Western Territories: Arizona, Colorado, New Mexico, and Utah*. Norman, Okla.: University of Oklahoma Press, 1959.

Commanger, Henry Steele and Milton Cantor, eds. *Documents of American History Volume 1 to 1898*. Englewood Cliffs, N.J.: Prentice Hall, 1988.

Connelly, Thomas. *Civil War Tennessee: Battles and Leaders.* Knoxville, Tenn.: University of Tennessee Press, 1979.

———. *The Marble Man: Robert E. Lee and His Image in American Society.* Baton Rouge: Louisiana State University Press, 1977.

Conrad, Robert. *General Scott and His Staff.* Manchester, N.H.: Ayer Publisher Co., 1977.

Coulter, E. Merton. *A History of the South.* Vol. VII, *The Confederate States of America 1861-1865.* Baton Rouge: Louisiana State University Press, 1959.

Davenport, Don. *In Lincoln's Footsteps: A Historical Guide to the Lincoln Sites in Illinois, Indiana, and Kentucky.* Black Earth, Wis.: Trails Media Group, Inc., 2002.

Davis, William C. *Look Away! A History of the Confederate States.* New York: The Free Press, 2003.

———. *The Cause Lost: Myths and Realities of the Confederacy.* Lawrence, Kans.: University Press of Kansas, 1996.

DeGregorio, William. *The Complete Book of U.S. Presidents.* New York: Wings Books, 1997.

Desjardin, Thomas. *These Honored Dead: How the Story of Gettysburg Shaped American Memory.* Cambridge, Mass.: DaCapo Press, 2003.

Eaton, Clement. *Jefferson Davis.* New York: The Free Press, 1973.

Eicher, David. *Gettysburg: The Definitive Illustrated History.* San Francisco: Chronicle Books, 2003.

Fahs, Alice. *The Imagined Civil War: Popular Literature of the North and South, 1861-1865.* Chapel Hill, N.C.: 2001.

Ferris, Norman. *Desperate Diplomacy: William H. Seward's Foreign Policy, 1861.* Knoxville, Tenn.: The University of Tennessee Press, 1976.

Fielding, Mantle. *Dictionary of American Painters, Sculptors and Engravers.* Greens Farms, Conn.: Modern Books and Crafts, Inc., 1926.

Foote, Shelby. *The Civil War: A Narrative.* 3 vols. New York: Random House, 1986.

Foulke, William. *Life of Oliver P. Morton.* New York: AMS Press Inc., 1977.

Freeman, Douglas Southall. *R. E. Lee, A Biography.* 4 vols. Safety Harbor, Fla.: Simon Publications Inc., 2001.

Frome, Keith W. and Richard Marius, eds. *The Columbia Book of Civil War Poetry: From Whitman to Walcot.* New York: Columbia University Press, 1994.

Gallagher, Gary, ed. *The First Day at Gettysburg: Essays on Confederate and Union Leadership.* Kent, Ohio: Kent State University Press, 1992.

Gragg, Rod. *Covered in Glory: The 26th North Carolina Infantry at the Battle of Gettysburg*. New York: HarperCollins, 2001.

Griffith, Paddy. *Battle Tactics of the Civil War*. New Haven, Conn.: Yale University Press, 1989.

Harris, Brayton. *Blue and Gray in Black and White: Newspapers in the Civil War*. Dulles, Va.: Brassey's Inc., 2000.

Hayne, Paul Hamilton. *Poems of Paul Hamilton Hayne*. Boston: D. Lothrop and Company, 1882.

Heard, Isaac. *History of the Sioux War and Massacre 1862 and 1863*. New York: Harper and Brothers, 1863.

Hendrick, Burton. *Lincoln's War Cabinet.* Boston: Little, Brown and Company, 1946.

Hill, Jim Dan. *Sea Dogs of the Sixties*. New York: A.S. Barnes & Co., 1961.

Hinze, David. *Battle of Carthage: Border War in Southeast Missouri*. Cambridge, Mass.: DaCapo Press, 2000.

Holden, Charles. "So Long's They Remember They Lost." *Columbiad* (spring 2000): 66-88.

Horowitz, Tony. *Confederates in the Attic: Dispatches from the Unfinished Civil War*. New York: Vintage Books, 1998.

Howard, William. *The Battle of Ball's Bluff*. Appomattox, Va.: H.E. Howard Inc., 1995.

Johnson, Clint. *Civil War Blunders*. Winston-Salem, N.C.: John F. Blair, 1997.

Johnson, Donald Bruce. *National Party Platforms*. 2 vols. Chicago: University of Illinois Press, 1966.

Joseph, Alvin. *The Civil War in the American West*. New York: Vintage Books, 1991.

Keenan, Jerry. *Great Sioux Uprising: Rebellion on the Plains, August-September 1862*. Cambridge, Mass.: DaCapo Press, 2003.

Kunitz, Stanley and Howard Haycraft, eds. *American Authors: 1600-1900: A Biographical Dictionary of American Literature*. New York: H.W. Wilson, 1938.

Landgon, Margaret. *Anna and the King of Siam*. Mattituck, NY: Amereon Ltd, 1944.

Lavender, David. *The Great West*. New York: Houghton Mifflin,1985.

Loewen, James. *Lies Across America: What Our Historic Sites Get Wrong*. New York: Touchstone Books, 1999.

Lowry, Thomas and Jack Welsh. *Tarnished Scalpels: The Court-Martials of Fifty Union Surgeons*. Mechanicsburg, Pa.: Stackpole Books, 2000.

Lucas, Charles. *Sherman and the Burning of Columbia*. Columbia, S.C.: University of South Carolina Press, 2000.

Higginson Book Company, ed. *Mankato, 1852-1902*. Salem, Mass.: Higginson Book Co., 1997.

McCaslin, Richard. *Tainted Breeze: The Great Hanging at Gainesville, Texas 1862*. Baton Rouge: Louisiana State University Press, 1997.

McElroy, John. *The Sacrificial Years: A Chronicle of Walt Whitman's Experiences in the Civil War*. Boston: David R. Godine, 1999.

McPherson, James. *Battle Cry of Freedom: The Civil War Era*. New York: Ballantine Books, 1988.

————. *Hallowed Ground: A Walk Through Gettysburg*. New York: Random House, 2003.

Miller, Edwin. *Selected Letters of Walt Whitman*. Iowa City, Iowa: University of Iowa Press, 1990.

Monaghan, Jay. *Civil War on the Western Border 1854-1865*. New York: Bonanza Books, 1955.

Moody, Edward. *Handbook History of the Town of York: From the Early Times to the Present*. Bowie, Md.: Heritage Books, 2000.

Moore, John C. *Missouri in the Civil War*. Wilmington, N.C.: Broadfoot Publishing Co., 1988.

Moore, Rayburn. *Paul Hamilton Hayne: Writer of the Republic*. New York: Irvington Publishers, 1972.

Morris, Roy. *Jr. Sheridan: The Life and Wars of General Phil Sheridan*. New York: Vintage Books, 1992.

Nye, Edgar W. *From Remarks by Bill Nye*. Chicago: Laird & Lee, 1892.

Painter, Franklin V. *Poets of the South*. Manchester, N.H.: Ayer Publishers Inc., 1977.

Palmer, Vera. "'Honest John' Letcher, War Governor." *Richmond Times-Dispatch*, January 13, 1935.

Patrick, Rembert. *Jefferson Davis and His Cabinet*. New York: AMS Press Inc., 1983.

Pfanz, Donald. *Richard S. Ewell: A Soldier's Life*. Chapel Hill, N.C.: University of North Carolina Press, 1998.

Phillips, Christopher. *Damn Yankee: The Life of Nathaniel Lyon*. Baton Rouge: Louisiana State University Press, 1996.

———. *Missouri's Confederate: Claiborne Fox Jackson and the Creation of Southern Identity in the Border West*. Columbia, Mo.: University of Missouri Press, 2000.

Pollard, William. *The Lost Cause: A New Southern History of the War of the Confederates*. Baltimore: E.B. Treat & Co., 1866. Reprint, New York: Gramercy Books, 1994.

Pope, John. *The Military Memoirs of General John Pope*. Chapel Hill, N.C.: University of North Carolina Press, 1998.

Ragan, Mark. *Submarine Warfare in the Civil War*. Cambridge, Mass.: DaCapo Press, 1999.

———. *The Hunley: Submarines, Sacrifice and Success in the Civil War*. Charleston, S.C.: Narwhal Publishing Inc., 1995.

Randall, J.G. *Lincoln the President: Midstream*. New York: Dodd, Mead, & Co., 1952.

Regan, Geoffrey. *Battles That Changed History*. London: Carlton Books Ltd., 2002.

Roosevelt, Theodore. "In the Louisiana Canebrakes." *Scribner's Magazine* (1908).

Rutherford, Mildred Lewis. *The South in History and Literature*. Atlanta: Franklin Turner Co., 1907.

Savage, Beth, ed. *African American Historic Places*. New York: Preservation Press, 1994.

Scott, William F. *The Story of a Cavalry Regiment: The Story of the Fourth Iowa Veteran Volunteers From Kansas to Georgia, 1861-1865*. Iowa City, Iowa: Press of the Camp Pope Bookshop, 1992.

Sears, Stephen. *George McClellan: The Young Napoleon*. New York: Ticknor & Fields, 1988.

Sherman, William T. *Memoirs of General William T. Sherman*. Westport, Conn.: Greenwood Publishing, 1972.

Silber, Nina. *Landmarks of the Civil War*. New York: Oxford University Press, 2003.

Silverman, Jason. *The Life and Wars of General Nathan Evans, CSA*. Cambridge, Mass.: DaCapo Press, 2002.

Stampp, Kenneth P. *Indiana Politics During the Civil War*. Bloomington, Ind.: Indiana University Press, 1978.

Stern, Philip Van Doren. *When the Guns Roared: World Aspects of the American Civil War*. Garden City, N.Y.: Doubleday and Co. Inc., 1965.

Sword, Wiley. *Shiloh: Bloody April*. Dayton, Ohio: Morningside House Inc., 1974.

———. *Southern Invincibility: A History of the Confederate Heart*. New York: St. Martin's Griffin, 1999.

Taylor, John. *William Henry Seward: Lincoln's Right Hand*. Dulles, Va.: 1996.

Thomas, Emory. *Robert E. Lee: A Biography*. W.W. Norton & Co., 1995.

———. *Travels to Hallowed Ground: A Historians Journey to the American Civil War*. Columbia, S.C.: University of South Carolina Press, 1987.

Trotter, William R. *Silk Flags and Cold Steel: The Civil War in North Carolina*. Wilmington, N.C.: John F. Blair Publisher, 1988.

Trudeau, Noah Andre. *Like Men of War: Black Troops in the Civil War 1862-1865*. New York: Little, Brown and Company, 1998.

Tucker, Glenn. *Zeb Vance: Champion of Personal Freedom*. New York: Bobbs Merrill Co., 1965.

U.S. War Department. *Official Records of the Union and Confederate Navies in the War of the Rebellion*. 30 vols. Washington D.C.: Government Printing Office, 1984-1922.

———. *The War of the Rebellion: A Compilation of the Official Records of the Union and Confederate Armies*. 128 vols. Washington D.C.: Government Printing Office, 1880-1901.

Utley, Robert, ed. *The American West*. 9 vols. Danbury, Conn.: Grolier Educational Corporation,1995.

Wagner, Margaret E., Gary W. Gallagher and Paul Finkelman, eds. *The Library of Congress Civil War Desk Reference*. New York: Simon and Schuster, 2002.

Wallace, Lee A., James I. Robertson, Jr. and Robert K. Krick, eds. *Southern Historical Society Papers*. 55 vols.. Wilmington, N.C.: Broadfoot Publishing Co., 1992.

Warner, Ezra. *Generals in Blue: Live of the Union Commanders*. Baton Rouge: Louisiana State University Press, 1964.

———. *Generals in Gray: Lives of the Confederate Commanders*. Baton Rouge: Louisiana State University Press, 1959.

Welsh, Jack. *Medical Histories of Confederate Generals*. Kent, Ohio: Kent State University Press, 1995.

Wheeler, Richard. *Sherman's March: An Eyewitness History of the Cruel Campaign That Helped End a Crueler War*. New York: Thomas Y. Crowell Publishers, 1978.

Whisker, James. *The United States Arsenal at Springfield, 1795-1865*. Lewiston, N.Y.: Edwin Mellen Press, 1997.

Williams, Harry T. *P.G.T. Beauregard: Napoleon in Gray*. Temecula, Calif.: Textbook Publishers, 2003.

Woodman, Harold, ed. *The Legacy of the American Civil War*. New York: John Wiley & Sons, 1973.

Woodworth, Steven. *Jefferson Davis and His Generals: The Failure of Confederate Command in the West*. Lawrence, Kans.: University Press of Kansas, 1990.

Wooster, Robert. *Civil War 100: A Ranking of the Most Influential People in the War Between the States*. Secaucus, N.J.: Citadel Press, 1998.

Wyeth, John. *The Life of General Nathan Bedford Forrest*. Edison, N.J.: Book Sales, Inc., 1996.

INDEX

al,

177

Antietam, 102-103
Appomattox, 114-115
Aroostook War, 58
Arsenal Monument, 170
Articles of War and Regulations of the Army, 131
Atlanta, Georgia, 91, 103-105

B

Bachelder, John, 161-162, 163, 166
Baker, Edward, 77-78
Banks, Nathaniel, 109-110

Battle of Chickamauga, 95
Battle of Glorieta Pass, 81, 97-98
Battle of Manassas, 93-95
Beauregard, P.G.T., 69, 71-73, 124, 151-155
Benjamin, Judah, 17, 24, 32, 38-40
Black Hawk War, 59, 67
Blair, Francis, 64
Blanchard, Enoch, 133
Boemer, Edward, 132-133
Bonham, Milledge, 20
Bragg, Braxton, 39, 72, 73-74, 151-155
Breckinridge, John C., 35-36
Briggs, Charles E., 140-141
Brown, Joseph E., 26-27
Buchanan, James, 33, 36-37, 64
Buckingham, William, 19
Buckner, Simon Bolivar, 96
Bulloch, James, 43
Bureau of Internal Revenue Service, 40
"Burial of Latane, The," 186-188
Burton, William, 25
Bushnell, David, 117
Butler, Benjamin, 26

C

Cameron, Simon, 17, 31, 37, 41-42
"Charleston at the Close of 1863,"
    190-191
Carroll, Charlie, 119
Chase, Salmon, 31, 37, 40-41
Cheeney, William, 118
Chickamauga, Battle of, 95
Civil War Dictionary, The, 100
Cobb, Thomas, 38, 94
Collier, Holt, 176-177
Columbia, South Carolina, 174-175
Commissary Department, 36
Confederate White House, 23-24
Conscription Act, 27
Cooke County, mass hangings at, 179-180
Cooke, Jay, 40
Cooper, Samuel, 64
Copse of Trees, The, 163-164
Craig, Henry K., 65
Crimean War, 43
Crisp, John, 180
Crittenden, George, 87-88
CSS Alabama, 44, 47
CSS Arkansas, 86
CSS Chicora, 123
CSS Florida, 44
CSS Georgia, 44
CSS H.L. Hunley, 123-125
CSS Indian Chief, 124
CSS Manassas, 119
CSS Rappahannock, 44
CSS Saint Patrick, 120
CSS Virginia, 23, 43, 121
Curtain, Andrew, 19
Custer, George Armstrong, 57, 68, 113

D

Davis, Jefferson, 17, 19, 20, 21, 23, 27, 31,
    32, 35-36, 38-39, 42, 45, 55, 67-76, 86,
    95, 97, 104, 108, 114-115, 169

Davis, Jefferson C., 79-80
Dayton, William, 31
de Villeroi, Brutus, 120-122
dead soldier poems, 185-187
Desjardin, Thomas, 164

E

Early, Jubal, 112-114
Eisenlord, Alonza, 134-135
Emancipation Proclamation, 19, 22, 25, 34
Evans, Nathan Shanks, 80-81
Ewell, Dick, 149-151
Explorer, the, 117-118

F

Fairbanks, Erastus, 20
Farragut, David, 98-99
Ferrero, Edward, 82
Five Forks, 105-106
Floyd, John B., 60
Flynn, Edward, 142143
Forrest, Nathan Bedford, 21, 148-149
Fort Donelson, 95-96
Fort George, 58
Fort Henry, 95
Fort Jackson, 26
Fort Pulaski, 26
Fort Sumter, 26, 33
Fox, Gustavus, 84-85
Freeman, Douglas Southall, 23
Fremont, Nathaniel, 109-110
Fulton, Robert, 117

G

Gardiner, Samuel, 65
Garnett, Richard, 154-155
Gettysburg, Battle of, 20, 22, 94, 161-170

Glorieta Pass, Battle of, 81, 97-98
Grant, Ulysses S., 17, 41, 95, 105, 111-115, 170

H

H.L. Hunley, 122-125
Halligan, John P., 120
Hammond, William, 139
Harney, William, 62-64
Harper's Weekly, 49
Harris, Isham, 87
Hayne, Paul Hamilton, 188-191
Hezlep, William B., 138-139
Hill, A.P., 99-101, 102-103
Hindman, Thomas, 39
HMS *Eagle*, 117
HMS *Pathfinder*, 125
Holmes, Theophilus, 39
Hood, John Bell, 55, 69, 75-76, 104
hospital fund, 131-132
Houdon, Jean-Antoine, 169
Hunt, Edward B., 119-120
Hutton, Eppa, 80-81, 154-155

I

Indianapolis Daily State Sentinel, 22
Intelligent Whale, the, 121

J

Jackson, Claiborne, 27-29, 64, 100-101
Jackson, Thomas J., 24, 39, 93, 109-110, 122, 167, 169
Japan, 47-48
Johnston, Albert Sidney, 95
Johnston, Joe, 57, 64, 69-71, 74-76, 103, 112, 155-156
Juarez, Benito, 45-46

K

Kansas-Nebraska Act, 35
Kemper, James, 154-155
Kirkwood, Samuel, 20
Kroehl, Julius, 117-118

L

Lakeman, William H., 137
Latane, William, 185-187
Ledlie, James, 81-82
Lee, Fitzhugh, 105
Lee, Robert E., 17, 20, 21, 24, 36, 60, 69, 70-71, 104, 108, 109-110, 114-115, 151-155, 167, 169
Legal Tender Act, 40
Letcher, John, 23-25
Lincoln, Abraham, 17, 19, 22, 25-26, 31, 37, 40-42, 59, 62, 66, 68, 77, 99-110, 172-177
Little Round Top, 164-166
Longstreet, James, 166-168
Loring, William, 24
Lyon, Nathaniel, 28, 64

M

Mallory, Stephen, 32, 43
Manassas, Battle of, 93-95
Mankato, mass hangings at, 178-180
Mason, James, 34
Mason-Dixon Line, 109
Maury, William, 44
McClellan, George, 37, 59, 62, 70-71, 94, 99-101, 102-103, 107-108, 109-110
McClintock, James, 122-125
McCulloch, Ben, 60
McDougal, David, 47-48
McDowell, Irvin, 93
McPherson, James, 94

Memminger, Christopher, 32
Merrimack, the, 23
Merritt, Wesley, 114
Mexican War, 58, 61, 67
Mexico, 45-46
Milton, John, 20
Mitchell, George H., 141-142
monuments, 161-180
Moore, Thomas, 20
Morton, Oliver P., 17, 22
Murdoch, James, 182

N

National Banking Act, 40
Nelson, General "Bull," 79
New Orleans, 98-99
New York City Draft Riot, 25-26
New York Times, 49
New York Tribune, 94
Newton, John, 83
Nicholls, Francis, 149-151
Norton, Oliver, 164-166

O

"Oh Captain! My Captain!," 194
Ordnance Department, 65

P

Pemberton, John, 111-112
Perry, Matthew, 47
Peters, Jessie, 86
Philadelphia, the, 121
Picket, George, 105, 169
Pickett's Charge, 154-155
Pierce, Franklin, 67
Pioneer, the, 122

Pioneer II, the, 123
poems, dead soldier, 185-187
Poland, 50-51
Polk, James, 36
Polk, Leonidas, 74
Pope Pius IX, 50-51
Porter, David Dixon, 111
Porter, Edward Alexander, 101
Provisional Army of the Confederate
    States, 68
Pruyn, Robert, 47

R

Read, Thomas, 181-185
Reagan, John, 32
Rienzi, 113, 183-185
Ripley, James, 65-66
Roanoke Island, 39
Roosevelt, Theodore, 47, 176-177
Rosecrans, William, 73
Rosser, Tom, 105
Rough and Ready Guards, 21
Ruffin, Edmund, 94
Russia, 48-50

S

Scott, Winfield, 57, 58-59, 64
Seldfridge, Thomas, 84-85
Seminole War, 62
Seven Days' Battle, 99-101
Seward, William, 17, 31, 32-35, 37, 44
Seymour, Horatio, 25-26, 41
Shenandoah Valley, 109-110, 112-114
Sheridan, Philip, 105, 113, 181-185
"Sheridan's Ride," 183-184
Sherman, William Tecumseh, 57, 103
Sibley, Henry, 97
Singer Submarine Corps, 122-125
Slidell, John, 34

Smith, Edmund Kirby, 69
Smith, Gustavas W., 70
Stanton, Edwin, 36-38
Stephens, Alexander, 32, 41
Stonewall Jackson, *see* Jackson, Thomas J.
Stuart, J.E.B., 94, 99-101, 169, 182
submarines, 117-125
Swamp Angel, 189, 191

T

Taylor, Zachary, 95
Tenure of Office Act, 38
Texas Secession Convention, 61
Thomas, Eli, 180
Thomas, Luther G., 135-136
Thompson, John Reuben, 185-187
Thompson, M. Jeff, 28
Toombs, Robert, 32, 42
Toon, Thomas Fenton, 145-146
Trent Affair, the, 34
Tucker, Glen, 21
Turtle, the 117-118
Twiggs, David, 59-61

U

U-21, 125
USS *Abraham Lincoln*, 121-122
USS *Alligator*, 84-85, 120-122
USS *Cairo*, 85
USS *Cumberland*, 84
USS *Housatonic*, 125
USS *Minnesota*, 118

USS *Octorara*, 120
USS *San Jacinto*, 34
USS *Santiago de Cuba*, 22
USS *Wyoming*, 47

V

Van Buren, Martin, 36
Van Dorn, Earl, 85-87
van Drebbel, Cornelius, 117
Vance, Zebulon, 17, 21-22
Vatican, the, 50-51
Vicksburg Campaign, 111-112
Vincent, Strong, 164-166

W

Walker, Leroy, 32, 35-36, 41
Walker, Lucius, 39
"War in Missouri in 1861, The," 29
War of 1812, 65
Warren, Gouvener K., 165
Watson, Baxtor, 122-125
Wheeling Convention, 107
Whitman, Walt, 192-194
Wilkes, Charles, 34
Wilkinson, Charles, 119
Wool, John, 61-62

Z

Zollicoffer, Felix, 87-88